Maternity Leavers

WHAT TO DO ABOUT WORK NOW YOU'RE A MUM

Soozi Baggs

DUX
PUBLISHING

ISBN: 978-1-911538-03-5

First published 2016

Copyright © 2016 Dux Enterprises Limited Trading as Dux Publishing.

All rights reserved. Apart from any permitted use under UK copyright law, no part of this publication may be reproduced or transmitted in any form or by any means, electronic or mechanical, including photocopying, recording, or any information, storage or retrieval system, without permission in writing from the publisher or under licence from the Copyright Licensing Agency Limited. Further details of such licenses (for reprographic reproduction) may be obtained from the Copyright Licensing Agency Ltd, Saffron House, 6-10 Kirby Street, London EC1N 8TS.

Printed in Great Britain for Dux Enterprises Limited Trading as Dux Publishing by Book Printing UK – Remus House – Coltsfoot Drive – Woodston – Peterborough – PE2 9BF

Copy-editor: Julia Kellaway – www.juliakellaway.co.uk
Cover and typesetting: Vanessa Mendozzi – www.vanessamendozzidesign.com

For A & R
This is Mummy's book

Throughout her working life, Soozi Baggs has tried many different jobs, always seeking the elusive 'dream career'. This quest has taken her from her first full-time job as an office clerk in Plymouth, to university in Wales, a brief teaching stint in Japan, and far too many years in London working in a secondary school, an international development charity and several law firms and financial institutions. After a few years of self-employment back in the sunny South West, she's now giving postgraduate study a whirl. As has been said on many occasions by friends and colleagues: 'If you're thinking of trying something different career-wise, speak to Soozi first – she's probably already done it.'

Soozi lives in south east Cornwall with her twin sons, where she writes and studies in 'Mummy's office' – the only room in the house not full of toys (although definitely full of paper and books).

Contents

INTRODUCTION — I
Why This Book? — III
Who Am I? — VIII

CHAPTER 1 - MAKING THE MOST OF MATERNITY LEAVE — 1
Assessing Your Options — 5

CHAPTER 2 - RETURNING TO WORK FULL-TIME — 9
Going Back to Your Old Job — 9
I don't know whether I want to go back — 10
I can't afford to go back with the cost of childcare — 12
I can't afford *not* to go back to work — 14
I'll miss my child growing up — 16
I'll be left behind after being off for so long — 18
What will my colleagues think of me now? — 20
What if I face discrimination? — 20
Make Your Return to Work Great — 21

CHAPTER 3 - FLEXIBLE WORKING — 29
Can I afford it? — 31
How do I approach my boss? — 33
My colleagues will resent me — 35
I'll never get promoted – I'll be stuck on the 'mummy track' — 36
How will I get everything done in less time? — 37
Everyone will think I'm less interested in my career — 38
What to do next — 39
Job Sharing — 43
Day-to-day realities — 46

CHAPTER 4 - BEING A FULL-TIME MUM   49
Coping with Kids Full-time   52
Make time for yourself   55
Your Relationship   56

CHAPTER 5 - SELF-EMPLOYMENT   61
Solopreneurs and Freelancing   65
Direct Sales   70
My experience   73
Franchising and Licensing   80
Retail and Selling Products   85
The Practicalities of Self-employment   95

CHAPTER 6 - DOING SOMETHING ELSE   101
Blogging   101
Podcasting   107
Writing a Book   110
Education and Retraining   118
Fears which might arise   122
Trading and Matched Betting   123

CHAPTER 7- MONEY AND PRACTICALITIES   133
Benefits   133
Shared Parental Leave   135
Childcare Solutions   137
Time Management   140
Investing in Yourself   147

CHAPTER 8 - MENTAL AND EMOTIONAL HEADSPACE   **151**

Mind-set   151
My experience   152
Motivation   154
What is your why?   156
Be Yourself   159
Your Relationship with Your Partner   162

CONCLUSION   **165**

RESOURCES   **169**

Introduction

WHY THIS BOOK?

Once upon a time being a 'stay-at-home mum' was just being a mum. If you had children, then you stayed at home to look after them. If you were rich, perhaps you had a nanny too, but you were the mum and your place was at home.

During the twentieth century gender roles started changing and relationships began to be seen more as equal partnerships. Women finally secured their right to vote in the 1920s and the 1970s brought the Equal Pay Act followed by the Employment Protection Act, which introduced statutory maternity leave of up to seven months, including pay for the first six weeks. Women were allowed to have jobs, leave them for several months to have a baby and then return to the same job. This was pretty ground-breaking.

Unhelpfully, this new-found liberation was billed as 'having it all' – having a job and having a family. The problem was that not everyone *wanted* it all. Some women wanted a career and no children, while others wanted a role as a housewife and to stay at home with their children. The former were often labelled as unemotional or not *proper* women and the latter were accused of setting the women's rights movement back decades. Somewhere in the middle were women who, instead of having it all, found they were just plain doing it all – navigating workplaces hostile to women (and especially towards those who were mothers) and then coming home to manage the majority of the housework and childcare.

These days employers are better held to account and there are more and more workplaces that go out of their way to welcome mothers back to the workforce after their maternity leave, making their work life at least that little bit more enjoyable. And although lots of mums still moan about dads being hopeless, we can hardly deny that it is becoming more acceptable for men to be home with their kids while women go out to work, and that lots of them are rising to the challenge and becoming more involved in both the parenting and the housework.

However, despite this progress, today in the twenty-first century there is still a battle raging between two sides. Not the familiar wrangling between couples over who's doing what household or parenting chore, but between those mothers who 'work' and those who 'stay at home'.

Social media is full of judgemental posts pitching working mums against stay-at-home mums. The comments threads are aggressive and anger-filled. If you've never read these posts about work-/family-related stuff, then do yourself a favour and don't. Who has it hardest? Who has the most tiring job? Is it harder work to work in an office away from your kids or to be at home with them all day? Who's the luckiest? Who feels sorry for whom? It seems many commenters think they're in a competition to win the Victim of the Year Award.

Social media threads like these show women reinforcing their right to feel like a victim; to feel like they didn't make the choice by their own free will, but that the choice was made for them. They didn't choose to work, they *had* to work. They didn't choose to stay at home, they *had* to stay at home.

You may never have seen or partaken in any of these arguments, so why do I mention it? Firstly because it illustrates that, sadly, the worst judgement most women get about their post maternity leave career choices is from other mums. And when it boils down to it, I want you to be aware of that so you can ignore that judgement.

Secondly, when you're making those career choices, it can seem like everyone is advising you what to do. Everyone has an opinion and many will drop that opinion into conversations when you didn't even ask for it. For instance, lots of people feel the need to defend their decision and do that by telling others that they should follow in their footsteps. Don't get drawn into other people's advice when you didn't explicitly ask for it.

And finally, lots of mums will sympathise with you that you don't have a choice – that 'going back to work' or 'staying at home' is your only option. Although they're only trying to help, it's unfortunately not a very helpful form of support. Because there are always options. And that is what this book is about. It's about finding and pursuing those options. It's about creating and crafting your future in such a way that you'll never be the kind of person who gets into a Facebook comments war on whether life is harder for full-time mums, or work-at-home mums, or work-in-an-office mums. You'll be making your own conscious choices on where your career goes from here, based on your dreams and ambitions, as well as who you are as an individual and as a parent.

I wrote this book because I want you to feel secure and happy with the choices you make. I've ended up trying a lot of different options in the six years since my twins were born. And every one of them was easier and harder than the others in some way. I don't pitch myself on either side of the debate because I've been on both (and other) sides of it and I've learnt there is no way better or worse than any other. It depends on you, your kids, your partner, your skillset, what work you do, and a million other variables. I've gone back to work and I've worked full-time inflexibly, flexibly, from home and part-time. I've also been a stay-at-home mum. I've been self-employed in a variety of different business ventures and now my kids are at school I've gone back to university.

Aside from my career details, in the last three years I've also got divorced and moved house with my kids to another part of the country. I understand reinventing yourself. I understand taking brave and difficult steps. And I understand what it takes to find another way when it feels like there are no options open to you.

Before you worry that I'm some kind of super mum, I'm not at all. I've struggled through many of the routes and life changes I've mentioned, and some have been less than successful. Throughout this book I draw on a lot of personal experience because I have plenty of it, which means I can share the stuff I learnt from messing up as well as offering advice I've gained from doing it well. I've also interviewed those who've made a success of it and have included their valuable tips throughout.

Above all I hope to show you that our careers after maternity leave are usually a combination of different options and that none of the choices you make are irreversible. Everything can be reviewed and changed if you need to.

Finally, I want to defend in advance why this book is for mums and not for parents in general. I have several male friends who have made good use of the extended paternity leave policies which have come into effect since 2011 and who share equally the domestic and parenting chores in their own homes. But I'm sad to say that, despite shared parental leave being introduced in 2015, they're still in the minority.

Yes, men sometimes have to make difficult decisions about their career after becoming parents, but there isn't the same societal pressure to make the choice between being a 'stay-at-home dad' or being a 'working dad'. In fact hardly anyone ever describes a man as a 'working dad' once he has a family, but being a 'working mum' always seems to crop up in discussions about women who progress to seniority in their career.

That's not to say there isn't any pressure on men – it's just not the same pressure. In fact, I welcome a book about men's choices after having kids. I'd love to read about what it's like to be a man who wants to take a bigger role in his family or who feels unsure about his career since becoming a dad. I know you guys are out there and you may even find something of use in this book, but I've written it for women because it's women who have to make these decisions every day and be judged by their families and strangers for the choices they've made.

I've outlined below a bit of my own background before moving on to why it's so important to use your maternity leave effectively, by reflecting on your career aims, so that you don't end up stumbling back to your old job without having thought through your other options. The book then moves through a range of ideas including returning to work, full-time mumming, starting a business, and others. You'll find explanations of what's involved in each option, together with some personal stories and a sprinkling of advice. Finally, I cover some aspects of money and practicalities, and your mental and emotional headspace, which apply whatever choice you make.

I mention some resources throughout the book, but as things change so quickly and websites come and go, I've mostly left out the specifics and will instead list links to resources on the Maternity Leavers website, which will be updated regularly: www.maternityleavers.com

WHO AM I?

I never thought I'd become a mum. I never really wanted children because I didn't get on with them particularly well and I couldn't imagine that I'd ever make a good parent. It wasn't because I had chosen my career over having children; I just saw them as two separate things that weren't linked.

I had heard people planning their career around babies (or

babies around their careers), of course. I worked with people who would say things like 'We're going to try for a baby this year because Graeme will have been promoted by the time it arrives and I'll be back in time to start on X project next year.' I was amazed every time I heard a conversation like that. Not in an appalled way, but because I could never imagine being organised enough to even think about planning a pregnancy so that the birth would happen in a particular month or quarter. It just struck me as being too impossible to even try. But then I used to baulk at the thought of committing to a definite night out with friends more than a week in advance. Planning and I don't mix. It's kind of ironic that I spent most of my twenties in jobs that included a lot of project management.

Around the beginning of 2010, aged 30 and married for a year, I could feel my attitudes shifting slightly. This was the time when I started to hear about friends having kids and when my Facebook news feed became less about hangovers and heroic nights out, and more about pregnancies and the horrors of being teetotal for nine months. At first it was unnerving seeing baby photos seemingly everywhere, but then I started wondering what it would be like to have a baby myself. And when I saw people younger than me having babies, it felt like the teenage race to start periods or to wear a bra all over again. I didn't really feel competitive though – it was something far, far worse. I was starting to feel broody. The thought terrified me so I decided to try and ignore it and see how I felt a few months down the line. Perhaps it would blow over.

I couldn't admit this to anyone. My carefully cultivated stance on being completely non-maternal wouldn't hold up to me discussing baby stuff with my friends. And my closest friends were nowhere near breeding, so it still wasn't a topic of conversation that came up much at the pub. But it did come up one lunchtime at work. A colleague had recently announced her pregnancy with her second and we got chatting about maternity pay over an asparagus risotto. I can still remember that chat, because it was one of those moments when you feel the bottom drop out of your world. Maternity leave and pay was not something I had paid much attention to. Perhaps I was more naive and optimistic than other more clued-up women, but I genuinely believed that maternity pay was pretty similar to your normal pay, just you weren't at work for 12 months or so. I think I picked up this idea in a previous job when a former manager went on maternity leave. We didn't discuss the ins and outs of pay, but I understood that she was being paid while off and that it wasn't that different to her normal pay. And when she decided not to come back, she waited until the appropriate time and then handed in her notice. At that point her pay stopped and she moved on with her other plans. Simple.

But it turns out that not every employer is this generous. And that statutory maternity pay is nothing like 'similar' to hardly anyone's normal salary. This chat with my colleague was eye-opening, because it turns out I was working for an employer who certainly wasn't going above and beyond, in a sector in which few rarely did. You'd think law firms would be generous (well, again, I did, but we've already established my embarrassing naivety on this front), but it turns out they're not. In the grand scheme of things, the maternity policy at the law firm where I worked was, it turns out, pretty good compared to many other similar firms. But it was stingy compared to every one of my friends and relations who had been or have since been on maternity leave. Not a scientific test, but good enough for me to feel hard done by.

You see, not being a planner, and not planning to have children particularly, I had not thought about where I would be working if the time came and what their maternity policy would be like. This chat with my colleague made it clear to me that there was no way I could afford to take maternity leave if I was still working at my current job. But since you usually have to be with an employer for a year or two before getting the full enhanced maternity pay package, I realised that even if I quit there and then and walked into another job at the end of my three-month notice period, I would be approaching my mid-thirties before I could even think about getting pregnant. And then what if it didn't happen right away?

It suddenly occurred to me what most women had probably realised a long time before me – that having babies seriously screws up your career. It dawned on me that the sheer time it takes to change jobs, and then settle for long enough to be entitled to the full package available, was the reason nobody else was job-hopping in the same way I was. Unfortunately,

I hated being stuck in jobs I hated and I was yet to find a job that I didn't hate. I wasn't strategic enough to work out when was the best time to have a baby in the middle of my ongoing quest for career nirvana (even career-mild-enjoyment would have done).

But the injustice of it all annoyed me. I couldn't shake this feeling that the whole maternity leave system in this country was based on the idea that a woman's salary is the second, less important, contribution to the family pot. A top-up of the man's substantial salary. Something that might be missed, but wasn't going to catapult a family into poverty were it to stop for a few months. Unlucky for me, then, that I'd always been the main breadwinner and that my salary was more than three times that of my husband's. Not that I was raking it in, but he was on minimum wage not even working full-time, and his monthly pay wouldn't even pay the rent, let alone the utility bills, food, travel and, oh shit, everything a baby needs.

At some point over the weeks following this conversation, while I was frantically looking for new jobs and trying to work out how you could tell how good the maternity pay would be before you even bothered applying for the job, I got pregnant. Not planned. Obviously. The universe's idea of a joke, I felt. And so, days after my 31st birthday, with financial panic ringing in my ears and a firm belief that I wasn't ready to be a mum in any way, I discovered I was pregnant. Scared shitless, but also, inexplicably, deliriously happy.

My husband and I had always said that if we ever had

children he would be a stay-at-home dad and I would work. I'm not sure how seriously I took this or how much thought I ever gave it – having children had always been a hypothetical thing after all. But financially it made sense and, actually, in other ways too. My husband had a head start on me in that he had actually held a baby. Several in fact. Coming from a large North African family and with three of his sisters already mothers, he was used to kids everywhere. I, by contrast, had never even seen a baby up close. I left the room when colleagues popped in with their new-borns at work. I knew nothing about babies and had no idea how to talk to or relate to kids. They made me nervous.

Aside from feeling short-changed on the maternity pay, I also felt annoyed over the length of time I'd have to stay in my job after returning to work. Leave before 12 months were up and I'd owe them a proportion of the money they paid me while I was off. Which meant not only had I been stuck in a job I hated for the past two years (thanks to the recession), I was going to have to come back to it and then stay a further year in order to avoid a financial penalty. Talk about staff retention under duress.

I told anyone who would listen about this injustice. Basically, I wanted out of this job and the timing of my pregnancy had made sure I was going to be there for the foreseeable future. In fact, if I took 12 months' leave, then went back for at least 12 months, I would have been there over four years, which far surpasses my longest serving job up until that point, which was around two and a half years. Four years felt like a life sentence, even if I'd be away from the office for a year of that.

Options were clearly something I didn't have. The plan became that I'd take a shortish maternity leave of about three months or so and then go back to work full-time. I felt it was all we'd be able to afford, and even that would be a struggle on half pay. After a year I'd hopefully find a job I would be happier in.

And then something threw it all up in the air. I went for my 12-week scan and, after some prodding around and far too many sharp intakes of breaths and furrowed brows – to the extent I was wondering what exactly was in there – the radiographer asked me if I knew I was having twins. I answered like any sane woman would – 'Are you kidding?!' – and then burst into tears. My plans for a short maternity leave went out the window as I wondered how on earth we were going to cope with twins, either practically or financially. And as two children would probably be enough, this would be my one and only maternity leave. Perhaps I should take a few more months off.

In the summer of 2010 my initial anger over the poor deal women faced over maternity leave was replaced by a laser targeted anger towards anyone on the packed commuter trains who didn't offer me a seat. I proudly sported my 'Baby on Board' badge and my twin bump was hard to mistake anyway. But it appears that all those badges do is encourage people to avoid all eye contact with you and pretend to be invisible. Or asleep. One morning I was roughly pushed out of the way when I was about to step on to a bus by a middle-aged man in a suit who was probably late for an incredibly important conference call. Commuting was one of the reasons I hated London and pregnant commuting, in the summer, was becoming a living hell.

For years, I'd wanted to leave London and the idea of raising my kids there was weighing on my mind. But where else could we go? This was where my job was and would be for the next two years at least. Part of me wanted to go back to my native Cornwall, but what would we do for money and work there? Jobs in my field of work – Knowledge Management and intranets – barely existed outside the M25. Unless, and it felt silly to even think it, let alone say it out loud, unless I worked for myself and mainly from home.

For weeks, the idea grew slowly until I couldn't ignore it anymore and I started buying books about freelancing and starting your own business. The seed of major life change had been planted – now I just had to work out how the hell to achieve it. The fact that it took me several years (and it's still an ongoing process) and lots of mistakes is what inspired me to write this book.

I hope that some of my experiences will inspire or inform you, whether you were born to be a mum or whether, like me, it was the last thing on your mind for most of your life.

CHAPTER 1

Making the Most of Maternity Leave

How many opportunities did you have in the past to really think about what you wanted to do when you grew up? Careers lessons at school? Hours spent on the Internet convincing yourself that you could really get excited about packaging because the graduate scheme paid a starting salary of over £25k and had a company car and extensive training programme included?

The truth is that most people give surprisingly little thought to their careers. I know people who are still in the same job they were in 10 years ago, not because they love it or have a desire to progress there, but because it's safe, secure and they've never thought about doing anything else. And maybe they're happy and it's all fine and everything. Or maybe they would actually benefit from a few months to a year off work, doing something completely different and thinking about whether they're really on the right track. Some people get that chance with a career break or a sabbatical. You'll get the opportunity with maternity leave.

For some career breaks people go trekking in the Amazon, building orphanages in Romania or teaching inner city kids to read. There are tons of personal development schemes out there where, if you've got a bit of time (and usually plenty of money), you can do something life-changing during your break from work.

So imagine, 12 months off work. A baby to care for, to bond with, to love, to cherish, to learn how to look after, to learn their special ways, how they're like other babies and how they're not. It definitely ticks the boxes of learning a new skill or doing something meaningful. On top of this you also get lots of time to think. There's plenty of sitting around, particularly in the early days when you need to rest and the baby still sleeps a lot. That stage doesn't last forever but you'll have a good few months before your baby gets really mobile. And walking is great for thinking, so you'll have plenty of chances to think while you're pushing a buggy around.

You might feel at first that you're too tired or busy to be soul-searching. Having a baby is a tough job and you'll probably be sleep-deprived and absolutely exhausted for the first month or so. Maybe longer. But there are two things to bear in mind here. One, even if you're tired and busy, you may be surprised how much time you have to yourself compared to when you were working a 40+-hour week. And two, it doesn't last forever. Potentially you have 12 months of maternity leave. You may even have a few weeks of it while you're still pregnant, so thinking about your career might be a better way to fill your time than watching daytime TV or reading yet another Mothercare catalogue.

You'll also hopefully find you suddenly have a lot of other new mums to talk to – many of whom are also thinking about their career. The good thing about people who don't know you very well is that they know nothing of your work identity, so chatting to them can be refreshing and unbiased. And depending on what life stage your other friends are at, perhaps you'll be on maternity leave at the same time as someone you know quite well and will have an opportunity to chat to them too. Whoever it is, use and value that talking time, although be careful not to use one person's opinion or advice to inform all your decisions.

On top of all the emotions and pressures of being a mum, you've now got to decide what to do about your job too. You probably started to feel differently about your life, job, career, yourself and your relationship when you found out you were pregnant. Then you have nine months of weird hormones and heart tugging firsts, followed by the birth where you may be overwhelmed with love for your little one and can't imagine leaving them to go off to work. Then you may be overwhelmed with all the work, the lack of sleep, the crying, and it may make you miss your job and want to get back as soon as possible. Both extremes are likely to be an unreliable barometer of your true feelings, so let it settle, take note of and recognise your feelings, but don't make any decisions yet. Acknowledge that this is a difficult decision made under emotional and ever-changing circumstances and that you may not feel fully ready to make the choice. Don't force yourself to decide anything too early. Obviously, you'll be bound by the practicalities of notice periods and other rules, but a good rule of thumb is not to commit to anything until you have to.

Talking and thinking is all very well. Even a bit of daydreaming is to be encouraged. But at some point, you'll want to commit pen to paper and start some planning too. Journaling about how you're feeling is a good place to start. If you've never journaled or kept a diary before you might find it a bit odd, but bear with me. Get a notebook or your computer (I've suggested a couple of good online journaling websites in the Resources section) and write down your thoughts or feelings about work. Don't overthink, edit, or keep reading back what you've written – give yourself permission to carry on despite spelling mistakes or not making sense. You're the only one who'll ever read it so it doesn't have to be perfectly polished, but you'll hopefully find that the act of writing your thoughts down will help you to clarify how you're feeling. Try writing something every day if you can, or at least with some regularity, and then after a few weeks or so, go back and read what you've written. It's interesting to see how your attitudes and feelings change from day to day or week to week, and also how ideas for solutions might pop up without you even noticing. If you were just thinking all this in your head, ideas can be easily dismissed or immediately forgotten, but when you're journaling, you have the opportunity to explore and assess these ideas because they're written down and less easy to ignore.

It's true that maternity leave is a time to bond with your baby. But doing something else for a few hours every so often doesn't mean you're not being an attentive mother. Other people will want to spend time with your baby – grandparents, your partner, other family and friends. Hand the baby over and enjoy some me time as often as feels comfortable. Some of that me time you'll need for pure relaxation – watch a film, read a book, sleep – but if you're feeling alert and introspective, use the time to work on yourself by writing in a journal, outlining potential business ideas, or reading a non-fiction book relevant to your career aspirations.

ASSESSING YOUR OPTIONS

You might think you've got far too many options for your future work life or you might feel you haven't got any wiggle room at all. Take a step back, relax and look for the positives in your situation. Try to objectively identify what options you have without getting bogged down by any negatives or feelings of despair. This book will help with ideas and by shining the light on the realities of what certain choices mean.

I want to add that none of these options are mutually exclusive. Most of us have chosen some combination of work, business and being at home with our kids. It's also important to remember that no choice once made is unchangeable. Circumstances alter, goals change and things just come up which means that what started out as a good decision that suited everyone becomes not quite right anymore, and things need to change. If that happens, be prepared to reassess and re-choose.

Even if you feel dead set on one particular option, have a read of the others anyway and see if there's anything you can incorporate into whatever decision you make. For instance, you may have an inkling that you want to start a business but it seems like such a big mountain while you're on maternity leave. But you lay some foundations anyway, by starting a blog, learning about marketing or building a presence on social media. You go back to work and a year later get pregnant again. This time around the mum stuff is easier because you've got experience of parenting and you're able to build on the work you did before in order to create a business which replaces your income and this time not return to your previous job. So, bear in mind the long game. There are decisions which are right for now, and there are decisions which take into account what you may want to do in future and which leave your options open in some way.

The chapters that follow will explore your options and help you to decide between them. Read through them all with an open mind. Suspend your preconceptions and consider each and every option as if it's a real possibility. Sure, every option won't be right for you, but you may surprise yourself which ones appeal to you when you open your mind to it.

CASE STUDY

Her story

I started working for CCM in 2003 at the age of 25 following a period of travelling and temp jobs after university. I worked hard and made my way up the career ladder from Business Assistant to Performance Manager, putting in long hours and travelling the country. I loved it! I married in 2006 and in 2009 I started to feel broody and that there might be more to life than work!

I was lucky to fall pregnant fairly quickly and in January 2010 I gave birth five weeks early to a gorgeous tiny baby boy. I hadn't even finished work properly so motherhood took over from my work routine without much thought. Fortunately, I was able to take 12 months' maternity leave and I thoroughly enjoyed my new role as a mother.

In discussions with my employer I approached the subject of reducing my hours. They were happy to accommodate my wishes and in January 2011 I returned to work three days a week. I felt I had a great balance. In addition, considering I had two female line managers, neither of whom had children, they were really understanding of my new life as a parent and any additional time I had to take off. I have friends who really struggled to get flexible working or reduced hours, especially within the teaching profession which always surprised me. It made me realise how lucky I was.

In 2013 I had a little girl. I took another 12 months off before returning to work but this time for three and a half days; all seemed good. But it started to get harder once my son started school in 2014 and school holidays came in to play. However flexible my employer was, I had a long commute due to the office moving and also our own house move and I started to feel I had lost my work–life balance. Having worked for the organisation for over 12 years, in October 2015 I took voluntary redundancy and decided to start my own business as a Virtual Assistant. It has been a steep learning curve but I am really happy with my decision as I feel my work now fits around my family life. I have now even started working one day a week on a self-employed basis for my previous employer.

Rachel Farrell
Virtual Assistant at Essential Business Support,
www.essentialbusinesssupport.com

CHAPTER 2

Returning to Work Full-time

GOING BACK TO YOUR OLD JOB

This seems to be the default position: get pregnant, have a baby and then go back to the same job. For many women this happens without much thought or planning. Your current job probably feels like the most sensible option – after all, who wants the hassle of starting a business or changing jobs at a time like this? Going back to your old job may be the right decision for you, of course, but make sure you throw the idea in the pot along with other ideas and subject it to a proper decision-making process. In other words, make the decision based on weighing up all your options, not because it looks like the only option.

Returning to work after you've had a baby is rarely easy and straightforward. A lot changes while you're on maternity leave; not only the practical side of having a baby, but your emotional and mental attitude too. You'll have fears and worries, new priorities, different income expectations and lots of other stuff swimming around in your head. Let's look at a few worries which may arise for you and how best to address them.

I DON'T KNOW WHETHER I WANT TO GO BACK

This is a common dilemma, but one which hides a multitude of reasoning, fears and underlying aspirations. What's your gut feeling? Do you like your job? Have you always liked it? Or have you always hated it and the thought of going back fills you with dread?

I strongly felt I didn't want to go back to my job because I had never liked it. On my first day back after maternity leave I had that sinking feeling that you get when you just know you've made a bad decision. But despite that and for a number of reasons (mainly thanks to a financial crisis and recession taking away the option of finding another job), I stuck with it for a couple of years with the plan to move on as soon as the chance arose.

In my situation, it was obvious that not going back would have been the ideal option for me (sadly that wasn't the decision I made, but that's a story for a bit later on). But what if your situation is not so cut and dried? What if you genuinely feel torn between staying or going and the fact that you're thinking of not going back actually surprises you?

First of all, allow yourself to feel the feelings. Imagine what it might feel like to go back or to leave. Let those feelings and thoughts percolate and develop naturally without trying to force a decision. Even I found some plus points to returning after I'd had a few months' break and motherhood had led me to a renewed ambition to advance in my career. Our attitude towards work can and does change constantly in the early months of parenthood. In the UK you're entitled to a whole year of maternity leave. If you're able to take the full amount, use the time to reflect on how you feel about returning to work in general, and your job in particular.

Journal about it, talk to your partner and really take time to explore how you feel. You might want to try a 'Pros' and 'Cons' list to help get your head straight on this. Journaling can help you explore your feelings by the act of writing them down, but sometimes you need the visual aid of a simple list to see what you like and don't like about a potential decision.

Those thoughts of 'I don't want to go back' or 'I think I do want to go back' are indicators of your aspirations. Don't stick your head in the sand and ignore them. If you can't shake the feeling of not wanting to go back, start researching your options and making some other plans. Even if you do end up ruling out other options, it's better to go back to work with the attitude that it's the best decision for you at this time, rather than a consolation prize because you didn't give yourself a chance to think of an alternative.

And if you're erring towards wanting to go back, keep in touch with your colleagues and make your feelings known. There are more ideas about the transition to work later in this chapter. The last thing you want is people making plans for your departure because you've given the impression of disinterest in coming back.

I CAN'T AFFORD TO GO BACK WITH THE COST OF CHILDCARE

There's no escaping this one. The cost of childcare in the UK is high – anything from £5,000 per year to £20,000 per year, depending on the type of childcare you choose and the region in which you live. Everyone goes on about it all the time, don't they? Yes, it's true that getting someone to look after your child is not cheap, but should it be? Childcare is hard, hard work and if you've decided to go back to work and leave your little one in the charge of someone else, don't you think you should be paying them well for it?

That may seem a bit harsh, but saying it's too expensive to go to work is an offhand comment that we use in this country far too often. I want you to feel less like a victim who's being fleeced by the system and more like a sensible grown up trading money for an important job. The media and other parents allow us to wallow in thoughts of 'Oh, but it costs so much money to go back to work because childcare is so expensive' that it's easy to forget the magnitude of what you're doing and why you're doing it. You're giving your child to someone else to care for while you work. There's no reason you should feel in any way guilty about doing that but paying to have someone look after your child, assuming they're doing it well, shouldn't be something you begrudge – it's a service of great value to you.

Whichever way you feel about it, the facts don't lie – childcare is a significant investment and should be a factor in your decision-making process. The simplest way to do this from scratch is to look online at a few nurseries and childminders or nannies and work out what their rates are. Work it out on a daily, weekly and monthly basis, and then work out what you get paid daily, weekly or monthly, and subtract the cost of working (e.g. commuting, buying lunch, etc.) and childcare. How much is left?

Now ask yourself two questions:
1. Is it worth doing my job for that much pay? Ask yourself whether you will feel resentful if you're working all day and bring home twenty quid 'profit'.
2. Is my career progression worth it? If you gave up your job and let yourself get out of touch with your chosen career for a few years, what would be the impact on your future career? Can you live with that or does that contribute to the worth and lessen the resentment in the first question?

Of course, the calculation you've done so far is a worst-case scenario. You may be entitled to benefits from either the government or your employer, or both. If you've done the calculation and found that the cost of childcare is more than what you earn then you'll almost certainly be eligible for some kind of help.) If the figure is too high, then it's a good starting point to think about flexible working, which is covered in the next chapter.

There's no doubt that working out the money stuff is a stressful time for most parents. But try not to fall into the mind-set of children being nothing but a financial drain. Very often the reality is that you can afford the childcare but you may have to give up some other things or find a way to earn more money – that's a reality of parenting in general. I talk about childcare in more detail in Chapter 5.

I CAN'T AFFORD *NOT* TO GO BACK TO WORK

This often comes coupled with the point before. 'Woe is me. Life is so hard – I can't afford to go to work but I can't afford not to…' and imagine the back of your hand pressed lightly against your forehead in a dramatic fashion.

I shouldn't make light of this though. It is the biggest fear for most women as the thought of not working, and therefore having no salary at all, doesn't bear thinking about. And for those of you who earn more than your partner, like I did, this will feel like a huge pressure on you. Again, do some basic calculations. Starting with your partner's income, take away the basic household outgoings, and see if you can live off what is left. Again, this would be a worst-case scenario because it assumes that you stop working entirely and bring in no money whatsoever, whereas in actuality, you might choose flexible working or self-employment, or possibly you may be entitled to some benefits.

Looking at your previous calculations, how much is your earning potential once childcare costs are taken out? This is the income level which you need to replace or do without – not the figures based on your double income before kids (that's no longer a reality).

This issue is obviously a practical one, but it's also a lot about mind-set and perception. Life changes after having a baby and, although I would never tell you that kids are cheap, be aware that what you spend your money on will almost certainly change. Things you may not spend so much on include socialising, smart clothes for work, daily travel and extortionately priced sandwiches. On balance, you might find that you can make do with less and the 'I can't afford not to work' may feel a bit of an exaggeration.

My first few months of maternity leave were spent frantically trying to work out if there was anything else I could do that would maintain my income but not involve me having to go back to work. Alas, I didn't find a way that would work before my time ran out. As the main earner in my household, once I got a few months into maternity leave and the 'enhanced pay' from my employer stopped, I couldn't see any option other than going back, no matter how much I didn't want to.

With hindsight, I'm still not sure I could have done anything differently, so if you're having this same dilemma, I really do understand how it feels. Sometimes, once you've done the maths, the fact remains that going back is the best option. The important thing for me was that I refused to be beaten by a decision I didn't want to make. I saw going back to work as only part of the choice and continued work on my longer-term goal which was to go self-employed when the time was right.

Above all, don't make this something you believe because it feels ingrained in you. I'm going to keep harping on about this but I want to make this point strongly. It's a decision that needs to be weighed up with lots of different factors. Going back to work on the basis of an ingrained belief of 'I can't afford not to work' is not based on an informed decision. Choices should be made with proper information, not vague assumptions. Besides, there are ways to make money other than through your old job and we'll explore these as we go through the book. Please keep an open mind.

I'LL MISS MY CHILD GROWING UP

This is another standard phrase that gets bandied around without much thought as to what it really means. Yes, if you work full-time that's a lot of hours a week that you're not with your child. But you know what, 'growing up' is about long-term presence. And parenting is about the effort you make to be present at the important milestones, and the not-so-important ones, and it's also about how you relish those milestones.

Just because you may not be around all day every day doesn't mean you'll be missing your child growing up. It just means you'll perhaps have to plan your time better to make the best of every second you've got. Even if you're at home you're not going to be giving your child 100 per cent attention for 24 hours a day. So, don't beat yourself up about not being there 24 hours a day. It's better to be attentive and focused on your child for a short time each day than to be at home with them all day thinking about how you really wanted to go back to work.

If you do decide to go back to work and then tell yourself constantly that you're missing them growing up, then that's how it'll feel for you. Tell yourself instead that you've decided to work in order to provide the best possible family life for your little one, then stick by your decision and make the best of it by spending as much time as possible with your child when you can. The only way you'll miss them growing up is if you go away, not by merely being out the house for a few hours a day.

It's important to look deeper too. This might be a strong belief to you and not just a platitude. If you really do feel that you're missing an element of them growing up, or you feel uncomfortable about them being looked after by someone other than you all day, then going back to work full-time might be something that doesn't suit you. Don't let anyone lead you into thinking that choosing to work full-time means you'll miss your children's childhood, but equally, if you feel uncomfortable being away from them for that many hours a week, be prepared to make alternative plans.

I'LL BE LEFT BEHIND AFTER BEING OFF FOR SO LONG

There's a myth that mums come back to work a shadow of their former selves, lacking in confidence, unable to do their fair share of work because they're constantly thinking about babies and generally not the employee they once were. What a load of crap! I haven't yet met a woman who became incapable of doing the job she left after a maternity break. And in the same way, I've never heard of anyone worrying that someone who's gone off on a sabbatical will come back less able. Assuming you were good at your job before you got pregnant, there's no reason why you should get left behind, and in fact, many women say they feel more focused on getting their work done and less distracted by office politics when being at work means not being with their baby.

However, things do happen in a year and systems move on. You may be faced with the struggle of a new IT system, for instance. Some companies introduce new systems and organisational change at an alarming rate (I should know – it's an approach which kept me in work for years). It's not unlikely that taking 12 months off will have you playing catch-up in certain areas. But don't assume that the people there will be dealing with it any better. And don't assume that it will put you at a disadvantage.

Situations like these can be minimised by keeping in touch with your employer and colleagues so you know what to expect on your return to work. Make use of Keeping in Touch (KIT) days throughout your maternity leave to attend training or spend time familiarising yourself with new systems or procedures. If you can't go in to the office, then at least ask your manager to let you know about major news and changes so you're not hit with it on the day you return.

If your fear of being left behind is more related to your industry than your job, try to read relevant articles, blogs and trade press while you're on maternity leave. Keep up with developments so you don't feel out of the loop. While you should absolutely think of yourself as being on leave, you don't have to think of your career as totally stopped. Unless you want to, of course.

In most jobs very little actually changes in a year. Sure you'll have to catch up, and that can take a little time, but people need to catch up when they come back from holiday. It's no big deal and doesn't mean you're 'behind'.

And a final note about confidence. Don't ever lose sight of why you have been off work for a whole year. You have become a mother. That isn't an easy transition. The experience and skills you've developed while you've been away will be of use to your employer. Rather than being 'left behind' you're the one who has come back refreshed, with a fresh pair of eyes to evaluate things that the people still there are too close to see properly. You'll probably be better at multitasking and time management than before you left, too. In short, you'll be a better version of the person who went away. So, what if you need a few days to get used to some new expenses procedure or random technology? You had a baby – everything else is easy.

WHAT WILL MY COLLEAGUES THINK OF ME NOW?

This worry also springs from a lack of confidence. Frankly, who cares what your colleagues think? So what if they decide you're going to come back all lost and behind – that gives you a chance to prove them otherwise. KIT days can be a great way of showing your intention to come back in full work mode. Keeping in touch with colleagues can also help with their transition – because that's what we're talking about here: *their* transition. You don't need to carry this all on your shoulders. They need to get used to you being around again, just as you need to get used to being there.

By the time you come back, don't forget, they will have been doing their job day in, day out for a year while you refreshed yourself and built a whole new life as a mother. They're probably going to be a bit jealous.

WHAT IF I FACE DISCRIMINATION?

Sadly, you'll need to be able to spot the signs of discrimination because it does happen and it's not uncommon. If colleagues, or worse, your boss, are obstructing you in your job or have taken away significant elements of your work to hand on to other people, then that's discrimination and needs to be dealt with.

Many instances are never reported because the woman finds it easier to switch jobs or just leave. Others go to HR or even legal tribunals. I can't advise on a hypothetical situation (or a real one actually since I'm not a lawyer) but this is the kind of thing that it doesn't do well to worry about in advance. If it happens, you should seek professional legal advice. The charity Maternity Action is a good place to start, whether you want to learn more about your rights or if you're worried that you're being treated unfairly (check the Resources section).

MAKE YOUR RETURN TO WORK GREAT

If you decide that you are going to return to your job, there are ways to make the transition easier, starting from the time before you even go on maternity leave.

Take control of your KIT days

Your employer may not talk much about your KIT days. Some women don't use them at all and many employers don't want to come across as being pushy by suggesting you come into the office when you'd rather be at home with your baby. So, if you want to make the most of these days, you'd better be the proactive one. Have a conversation with your manager before you even start maternity leave so they know your intention to make use of your entitlement, and then email or call them to discuss it further nearer the time you actually want to come in. You're paid at your normal daily rate for each KIT day used (even if you don't work for the entire day) and you can spread these 10 days throughout the entire 12 months of maternity leave, or however long you're off for, so think about how you can stagger them to work out best for you.

If one of your fears is getting left behind, particularly if you know there's a new system or process being implemented while you're off, you could use a KIT day to come in for a training session. If you can organise this to be on the same day as the rest of your team, all the better, but even an ad hoc session with a team member will keep you up to speed and demonstrate your willingness to come back ready to work.

Another idea might be to attend a meeting that you feel is important or relevant. Perhaps a departmental one that only happens every few months or a company-wide meeting that only happens once a year. A team away day is another good one, especially if the focus of the day is planning for the next year or looking at the team strategy. That's exactly the kind of event where you want to get your thoughts and opinions heard, especially if you're working towards a promotion. And if you love formal appraisals (and who doesn't) you may want to use a KIT day to pop in for yours. This has the added bonus of giving you formal objectives to come back to when you return.

Above all, KIT days give you visibility and a chance to demonstrate that you're looking forward to coming back.

Keep in touch with your colleagues

This doesn't have to be anything formal – that's what paid KIT days are for. If you're already friends with colleagues on social media or you exchange the odd email, then you don't need anyone to tell you to carry on doing it. Just keeping up this brief contact may be enough to alert you when any developments arise – perhaps someone else is now pregnant, or leaving, or has been promoted, leaving an opportunity open for you.

Rightly or wrongly, we all know that lots of opportunities and progressions are made based on who you know and what you learn at the water cooler. It's the same principle here. Keeping your ear to the ground is good advice whether you're on maternity leave or in the office every day. So, keep having those conversations with your colleagues. It'll also have the added benefit of stopping you feeling cut off from the world (as many women do after giving birth) and maintaining your identity as a *[insert job title here]* as well as a 'new mum'.

Read voraciously

You know how, when you're at work, you get sent links to articles you never quite find the time to read or industry updates which you skim through without taking anything in? Because you're so busy doing your day-to-day work, having the time to read around your topic is a luxury that no one actually has. There are trade magazines for almost every conceivable industry – from pencils to paper clips – but whoever sits at their desk reading one? Even though it's highly relevant, just sitting there reading feels like you're 'not working'.

The great news is that when you're on maternity leave, you have the chance to catch up on all this reading and learning. You're still in your career, you're still interested in this stuff and you actually have time to read it because no one is bombarding you with the day-to-day minutiae. And reading is one of the few activities that is very easy to do while you're breastfeeding or sat on the sofa acting as a pillow for a snoozing baby.

Imagine how knowledgeable you'll be when you return to work. You can quite literally be the fountain of all industry-related knowledge for your colleagues who haven't had the same chance.

Create a new CV

I know, groan. But trust me, this is meant to be a fun exercise. I don't mean create a new version of your old CV; I'm talking about creating a 'Mum CV'. This is great thing to do if you're ever feeling a bit overwhelmed by parenting and having one of those familiar moments we all have when we think we're no good at this and, by extension, also crap at everything else. (If you never feel like that, then you're very lucky and will find this exercise super easy.) You definitely need to do this if you've ever worried that becoming a mum will make you worse at your day job.

In the section at the top where you say what your job title is, put that you're a mum. In the skills section, put in all the skills you can think of related to being a mum: 'I can change a nappy in under 15 seconds', 'I can remember all the words to Puff the Magic Dragon and sing it when I'm sleep-deprived', and so on. No one else needs to see this so you can be as tongue-in-cheek as you like. The aim of the exercise is to show you all the new things you've learnt in a short space of time and give you a confidence boost when you need it most.

You may well find some skills on there that are completely transferable to your proper CV: 'I can get two toddlers fed, nappy changed and dressed with scarves, gloves, coats, hats, welly boots, then out the door and into a buggy in less than 20 minutes' becomes 'I am a logistical expert who deals calmly with objections and challenges to make sure that all staff contribute to achieving the organisation's aims.'

You could do this exercise every couple of months while you're on maternity leave because babies develop so quickly that your learning and new skills quickly mount up.

The final point I want to make is that being a mum enhances the skills you had before – it doesn't take them away. If you decide to return to work then your employer should realise how lucky they are to get you back, so don't ever feel like they're doing you a favour by holding your job open.

Find a New Job

Finding a new job is always a bit of an upheaval and, let's face it, a bit of a risk too. While you know the lay of the land at your current job, even when there are parts you don't like, a new job is a bit of a mystery. In fact, a lot of people stay where they are not because they love their job but because it's familiar – they know what's expected of them, they know what they can get away with and they like their colleagues. Unless you're very ambitious or very unhappy where you are, getting a new job may not have occurred to you, but since you're going through changes anyway as a result of becoming a parent, it might actually be a good time to look at changing your job too.

Just before I returned to work after seven months of maternity leave, a new position came up at a global consulting firm. The position was similar to what I was doing at my previous job, but crucially for me it was part of a bigger team, with a greater chance of promotion (in my existing job there wasn't really anywhere to be promoted to). I applied for the job while I was still on maternity leave and got invited for interview during my first week back. Following that interview and a second one a week later I was offered the job.

As it happens I didn't take the job in the end as the salary on offer didn't match my expectations and would have put me in a worse financial position, thanks to my employer's requirement that I pay back my enhanced maternity pay if I left within 12 months of returning. (I know my ex-employer has since scrapped that requirement, but it's worth checking if there is any similar clause in your own maternity leave policy.)

But whether I took the job or not, the bit I want to focus on is that I was offered the job and that boosted my confidence greatly. I found that the time I'd had on maternity leave made me more ambitious and more determined to increase my salary for the sake of my family. It also made me aspire to work in a job that I felt was meaningful and where I was a valued member of the team (I had felt anything but at my previous job). Lots of women have a rocky return to work because they're going back to the same job with the same colleagues and yet they've changed. Sometimes it's not the fact that working is wrong for us, it's the fact that we've outgrown our previous role.

I don't think I need to go into detail about how to find or apply for a job, except to say that if you're looking for flexibility in your work then use a job search website that is aimed at working parents. The employers who advertise there will be more likely to offer family-friendly policies and be open to flexible working or job shares (see Chapter 3 for more on this).

I'd hope you would update your CV before applying for a job anyway, but have a think of any skills you can add to it that you've gained since becoming a parent (you don't have to say this is how you learnt the skill) or any relevant work or training you did while you were off. And bear in mind that you don't have to state that you have been or are on maternity leave when you list your work history – maternity leave is not a break in employment so you don't have to record it as one.

If a job comes up that you'd like to apply for while you're in the middle of (or even beginning) maternity leave, apply for it. I know of people who have negotiated a start date several months down the line because they were the right person for the job and the new employer was prepared to wait for them to be available. Don't assume that if you're not ready to start right away then they won't want you. If you do end up having to compromise and shave time off your maternity leave then that may be a small price to pay to be in a job which suits you better, or is more flexible, than your old one.

Finally, I'm often surprised by how loyal some people are to their current employers, even when they've been treated poorly by them in the past. Your employer pays you for your work but beyond that you don't owe them anything. Even if your manager is lovely or you feel an obligation to stay because they paid you while you were on maternity leave, those are not good reasons to stay if the job doesn't otherwise fit in with your new family life. Your colleagues may be sad to see you go but they'll get over it. Staying at your job or taking on a new one are choices which are entirely yours to make. It may sound harsh, but you should rarely have to take other people's feelings into account when making that choice.

Going back to work full-time doesn't suit everyone, so it's worth exploring flexible working or even job sharing. I'll deal with this in detail in the next chapter.

CHAPTER 3

Flexible Working

Dagger looks and knowing glances pass around the office as a working mum stands up at 4pm and puts on her coat. It doesn't matter that she was at her desk before 8am (over an hour and a half before the rest of the office trickled in). No, leaving at 4pm is 'lucky' or 'lazy' or downright 'cheeky'.

If you want to work flexibly, you might have to get used to this attitude, because as long as people are forced into working 9–5 or other standard hours from their office, there will be resentment towards those who manage to negotiate themselves a more flexible way of working. However, flexible working is becoming more mainstream and, thanks to technology, the opportunities for remote working are far more prevalent than they used to be. Hopefully then, scenes like this will become a thing of the past.

At its heart, flexible working is really about giving employees a bit of freedom and autonomy; to trust them to deliver results rather than measuring them on how many hours they're sat at their desk. It's what every worker would love to have, whether they're a parent or not. And in fact, by law, every worker has the right to apply, but it tends to be parents who make the majority of applications.

So what exactly is 'flexible working'?
There are three main flavours:

1. Changing the number of hours you work. Typically this would be to reduce the number of hours you work in a week, from say 40 to 30, or whatever.
2. Varying the times that you work. You would normally work the same number of hours over a week, but work them in a different pattern. For instance, you may want to do compressed hours – work longer days but only come in four days instead of five, while still maintaining the total number of hours over the whole week. Or simply starting and finishing earlier or later in order to fit in with other commitments such as childcare or school pick ups and drop offs.
3. Changing your place of work. The most common one would be to work from home for an agreed number of hours/days per week.

Those employers that are inherently traditional and after an easy life would obviously prefer it if you just stuck to what you've always done and worked the same hours as everyone else. It makes life easier for them when everyone knows what everyone else is doing and when they're in. The great thing is that lots of offices aren't like this anymore. Teams are a combination of different working hours and people working from home, either regularly or at least from time to time. Technology means we don't need to be in an office all day any more. People can send and receive work, and appear at meetings remotely.

So let's look at the practicalities of flexible working. Because most employers' default position seems to be to look for holes or flaws in order to reject your request, you must not make it lightly or apologetically. Face them head-on and tell them how they're going to benefit from you working more flexibly. You are making a business case – treat it like one. We'll go into more detail about putting that business case together later in the chapter, but first I can hear those voices in your head hollering with their woes and worries, so let's address these first.

CAN I AFFORD IT?

Money – the big worry for us all. When most people think about flexible working they think they have to go part-time and therefore take a drop in salary. Perhaps you do want to go part-time, but there are also other options which don't affect your income.

Flexible working means that you could suggest a way of

working the same number of hours as you do now but at different times. If you've always worked 9–5, why not think about 8–4? Maybe you want more flexibility in the afternoon so you can spend time with your baby before bedtime or maybe, since you're going to be up early anyway, it makes sense to get the day started as soon as possible.

Compressed hours allow you to work your weekly hours over four days instead of five so that you get a three-day weekend, and it's only a couple of extra hours each day. Some companies will even allow you to annualise your hours, spreading your working hours over a year rather than a week and allowing you to be really flexible, usually within the confines of core hours.

For a lot of parents who work the biggest issue is getting to the nursery in time for pick up. If you find your commute time means that your working day is longer than your nursery's you might want to apply to work from home several days a week. If you can balance this with your partner doing the same you might be able to cover the whole week between you.

Though flexible working doesn't have to mean part-time, you may want it to. And then the question of money goes back to the calculations I went through in Chapter 2. Calculate how much less money you'll get and work out if it's worth it for the additional time you gain. Although most of you will be planning to use any time off work to be at home with your baby, there's also the option to go part-time at your job as a way of building up a freelance business. So, you may still be working full-time hours overall, but you'll be paving the way to working for yourself and being as flexible as you want to be in the future.

HOW DO I APPROACH MY BOSS?

Honestly for a start. Start discussing that you're interested in flexible working as early as you feel comfortable. It gets the idea out there which gives your boss more time to consider how it might work. Sometimes managers need to mull over this kind of request for a while to see how it sits with the rest of the team. If your boss is a thinker, then give them time to think. It's worth bearing in mind that a formal request for flexible working can only be made once a year, so check out the lie of the land and put in your application *after* discussion with your manager, not before.

If you are looking for proper part-time working, rather than variations to your hours without an overall reduction, be realistic about what you're asking for. Think about how this will impact your boss and what they are responsible for. They've got one person working 40 hours at the moment. If you start working 30 hours, they're losing 10 hours a week, and very often they're not going to be able to employ anyone else to do that work. The letter that supports your application must include an explanation of how you think your new working pattern will affect the business, so you need to address all your employer's potential objections in that letter.

Establishing the benefit to all parties is the key to all negotiation, I believe. I spent many years preparing and supporting people through organisational change and the same principles apply to individual change. Find the benefits for all the parties involved and the request is more likely to be approved. So, benefits to your employer might include increased staff cover at certain times (if you're suggesting starting earlier, for instance) or even reduced staff cover (and therefore reduced staff costs) at times when it's quiet anyway.

If your application is approved, adjustment time will be necessary, so don't treat it as an afterthought. How you and your colleagues should smoothly adjust and the expected timescale for doing so should be included in the application. After all, you wouldn't normally suggest a project without some idea of how long it's going to take. In order to take the personal out of your request, treat it as you would a project approval (or whatever your equivalent is). You're putting forward a case for something which you feel will add benefit. State your case as factually as possible and then leave it in the hands of the decision maker. If you take the personal out of it, then hopefully your boss will too and the decision made will be fairer.

Of course, bosses and employers come in all flavours and only you know the quirks and foibles you may be up against. There is no doubt that this won't be easy for everyone, no matter how business-focused the application procedure. Some bosses are complete arses. That's when it pays to know your rights and to do everything completely by the book. The Maternity Action website has lots of information on your rights and what to do if you feel you've been discriminated against.

MY COLLEAGUES WILL RESENT ME

They may well do, but why should that matter to you? Put yourself in their shoes. Perhaps they don't like their job that much or they're jealous of your seniority, or whatever. If you are then allowed to work fewer hours or turn up and go home when you want, of course it's going to rock their boat a little bit. From their point of view, someone is getting an easier ride than them and they may not like that.

However, if this particular person isn't rushing home from work to pick up their child from nursery, cook dinner and then pop the little one to bed via a bath, then, to them, being able to leave work an hour earlier than everyone else probably seems like a bit of a luxury. You, however, know the truth – that it's simply a necessity to manage all your responsibilities.

I guess what I'm saying here is, you're entitled to apply to work flexibly. Don't let anyone guilt trip you into not applying or watering down the request.

I'LL NEVER GET PROMOTED – I'LL BE STUCK ON THE 'MUMMY TRACK'

Ah, the 'mummy track'. If you've never heard the term, it describes the situation where a woman feels she's been pushed into a slower career progression because she's working reduced or flexible hours. Although somewhat intangible, the mummy track does unfortunately seem to be very real. Like with your chances of getting flexible working in the first place, a lot depends on your employer, their family policies and their general attitude towards women.

The mummy track is really just another form of discrimination against women, but it's not always easy to pinpoint exactly in what form the discrimination is taking place. For instance, not getting promoted could feel like it's because you're a mum, but your employer could argue it's because you're not yet ready; it's very hard to prove that's discrimination.

It's impossible to advise how to escape the mummy track as it will apply to everyone differently, but there are a few things you can do to lessen the impact and stop it happening to you.

1. Once your flexible hours have been agreed, stick to them.
2. Do your job well.
3. When you're at work, be present. Show you're committed and keep personal calls and errands to a minimum.
4. Use your appraisal process to demonstrate that you're still ambitious, committed and looking for promotion, and that you're fully able to take on more responsibility.

Above all, do what you've always done to get where you are today and make it clear that, although you're a mother, flexible working is purely about allowing time to fit in everything you need to do – it doesn't mean you are any less committed to your job.

The last thing to say is that not all organisations have a mummy track. Some have excellent family-friendly policies and see the value of employing workers who are parents too. If your place of work is not like this, then it may be time to start considering moving elsewhere if you want to continue climbing that ladder. The problem isn't with you – it's with them – but sometimes the best way to challenge it is to take your value somewhere else.

HOW WILL I GET EVERYTHING DONE IN LESS TIME?

You won't, unless you're planning to damage your health and be a martyr. That's why, if you're planning to reduce your hours, you should be reducing your workload too. This should be part of the plan you put forward. Give it a lot of thought. Start looking now at what your daily tasks are and how long they take. If you're going to cut, say, 10 hours out of your week, what tasks could you no longer perform?

This is really the nub of the negotiation, because this is the part where you're clearly saying that there are some things you will no longer be able to do, and those things will either not get done or someone else will have to do them. And that's your employer's problem to solve.

Don't allow this to be glossed over. If they agree to drop your hours but are dismissive about who is going to do that work, the reality is that it'll be sat on your desk jostling for your now limited time. You don't need the added stress of feeling guilty about work which should not now be your responsibility (and which you're no longer being paid to do). Make sure this is addressed before you start your amended work pattern, because once you have started it, if you're seen to be 'not managing' your workload you may lose your right to flexible working.

EVERYONE WILL THINK I'M LESS INTERESTED IN MY CAREER

Who is 'everyone'? Your colleagues? Your boss? Your partner? Your mum? Who of those people matter? What do they really think?

What other people think isn't really important, unless it's causing them to cross boundaries of discrimination at work. If your colleagues are excluding you from relevant meetings or placing unreasonable pressure on you to complete something for which you don't have the time, then this could be discrimination and you should speak to HR, your boss or your union about it. But if it's just people having a general feeling that you're less interested, who cares? Your 'career' is a personal thing. How you choose to progress it is up to you. As it happens, many women who have gone back to work after having children have done so out of choice, precisely because they are committed to their career. They're making the choice to leave their children for several hours a day in order to do their job because it's important to them. Those women value their career highly and demonstrate that by continuing with it after becoming a parent. Be confident in your decision to return to work and don't let others make you feel inadequate.

Flexible working is not a weakness and is not a demonstration of reduced commitment to your job. Rather, it's a sensible way to reorganise your working day around your additional responsibilities. The only people who are likely to see it as anything other than that are those who are jealous that you're more than capable of organising a complex life when all they manage to do after work is sit in the pub with a pint or go home and watch EastEnders.

And you know what, if you are less committed to your job, that's okay too. Perhaps after returning to work for a bit you'll find that you do feel differently about your career. And maybe you'll decide that it is time to move on in some way. A career change, self-employment or a period as a full-time mum … there are plenty of other options if you find the spark has gone.

WHAT TO DO NEXT

Do some informal research by checking out the family policies on your intranet or in your employee handbook. Are other people in your organisation, your department or your team working flexibly due to family commitments? If so, your employer is more likely to be open to it (but be careful about clashing – someone else in your team may be able to leave early only because you currently do not, for instance). If you're comfortable enough to do so, ask someone how the process was for them. Did the employer make it difficult or was it fairly laid-back and the application just a formality? Look at the different types of flexible working. Which one do you think you'll apply for? Discuss it with your partner and find out what's available where he works too.

If you've taken a whole year off, then make sure you familiarise yourself with the dynamics of the team before you make your application. Who has left or arrived since you've been off? What working pattern is everyone else on? KIT days are useful for getting back up to speed, meeting new team members and generally doing some poking around, so you may want to save a couple up to use in your final month of leave.

In the spirit of getting the lie of the land before making your move, an informal way to work flexibly while easing yourself in gently, is to use your accrued leave days spread over several weeks (if your employer agrees it). If you're off for a year, you could accrue around a month's worth of holiday (depending on your entitlement, obviously) so you could work 'pretend' part-time, taking two days off a week, for a month or two. I did something similar to this for my first month back. If you're planning on going part-time, this would allow you to see how part-time feels as well as giving you time to make your application the best it can be.

Even if you don't intend to work part-time ultimately, the shock of going from maternity leave to a five-day working week is pretty intense, so do consider using your holiday entitlement to do this phased approach. Another option is using it for a thirteenth month of maternity leave. However, although this may feel nice at the time, it's really only putting off the inevitable and if you're that unkeen to return, perhaps you should be considering other options rather than postponing the agony!

CASE STUDY

Her story

Before going on maternity leave I was working in two overlapping roles for the same company. They agreed that I could return to just one of the roles working part-time, three days a week.

Before I told them I was pregnant we discussed a discretionary pay rise at the end of the year, when I was due to be on maternity leave. They honoured it, which I thought was decent of them. In the 18 months after returning, I had two further pay rises and a promotion.

It was challenging at times making the role work in just three days and juggling it with pick ups and drop offs; I did often have to do work at home or take calls on my day off, but my company were very understanding about me leaving on time and having commitments outside of work. Ultimately it was a good balance with plenty of give and take and I appreciated that my ambition and hard work were recognised and rewarded even though I was working part-time.

Anonymous

JOB SHARING

A surprising number of people I've spoken to think that job sharing is an urban myth. They've heard of it, but don't know anyone who does it. Job sharing is technically just a type of flexible working, but it's different to any other form of flexible working, in that it includes another person. Job sharing is an option that a lot of people never even consider, so I think it's important to go into a bit of detail about it here.

My first experience of seeing a job share at work was when I was temping for my local council not long after leaving university. I was in the social services department and there were two women who job shared there. One did Monday to Wednesday; the other Wednesday to Friday. The day they were both in the office they exchanged notes, went to meetings together and planned how the next week was going to pan out. I remember thinking what a lot of organisation it took for them to make it work, but how good it was that they both got to work only three days a week.

Funnily enough, in all my jobs since (and there have been quite a few) I haven't come across any other job shares, or at least none that I noticed or was close enough to see working. But it's one of those things that if you start looking for it, you'll find plenty, and such was the case when I decided I was going to include a section on it in this book.

Perhaps my biggest discovery during research was that the civil service now has a 'job share finder' where you can search for suitable job share candidates: people who are qualified for the same jobs as you and who are also looking for a job share. You then form a partnership with that person and apply for jobs together.

There are two big advantages to job sharing over part-time working – one for you and one for your employer:

1. In contrast to part-time working, your job remains at a full-time level. This is great for your employer because it means that they don't have to get any special approvals from their management or rethink the workload of the role, as they would if they were regrading it as part-time. They don't lose anything and, in fact, they gain two heads working on the same job. When putting forward your case for job sharing, these benefits are something to focus on.
2. Although you're working part-time, your work is continuing on a full-time basis, which means that you won't have half a week of emails and queries to catch up on when you come in at the start of your week. Things will have moved forward while you've been off and you can just pick up where your job share left off.

Because job sharing is still seen as one of those new-fangled innovative ideas, most people's questions and fears are around the practicalities. How on earth does it work …?

Choosing the right job share partner

Not all job shares work in the same way, so how best to set it up varies. As I mentioned previously, large organisations, such as the civil service, may have a database where you can look for someone suitable internally and set up the partnership before you apply for your own job to become a job share (or apply for a new job together). Even if there is no formal procedure available, you may have someone in mind either from within or outside of your organisation, and can agree with them to approach your employer with the proposal of the two of you job sharing. If you're open to the idea of changing roles rather than converting your old job to a job share, you can filter by job shares on most job search websites, especially those aimed at working mums.

The good news for you is that job sharing comes under the banner of flexible working, and you have a statutory right to request flexible working and for your employer to consider your application. That said, in order to encourage your employer to accept your application, you'll want to be as accommodating as possible, so the groundwork of finding a suitable partner will fall mainly with you.

In terms of who will make your ideal job share partner, there are obvious things to consider like the right qualifications, ability and experience to do the job, but beyond that it's down to personal choice. You must be able to work with this person, and you need to be comfortable passing work on to them to finish and taking over work that they've started.

That means you should have faith in their abilities and gel with their working style. There's also likely to be compromise needed on both sides and a willingness to go out of your way (within reason) to help the other. By which I mean things like not leaving stuff until the last minute and not doing all the easy tasks, leaving the harder ones for them.

It also helps if you have similar career aspirations. You don't want to settle in to a new job share arrangement only for your partner to announce before you're ready that they're looking for promotion. Likewise, you don't want to feel held back by a job share partner who has no ambition to progress when you do.

DAY-TO-DAY REALITIES

How many hours each of you works, and on which days, is ultimately decided during a negotiation phase with your employer. The most popular pattern seems to be three days each with one day overlapping. That way the employer is getting six days' work instead of five and you both have the opportunity to work together regularly and do a weekly handover.

There's bound to be a bit more of a settling in period with a job share than with someone just starting a new job or returning to their old one. Both sharers need to be comfortable with who is doing which tasks and when, and how the issue of communication with the immediate team, the organisation and clients will work. For instance, will you work from a single email address which you both monitor or do people need to copy both of you in on each email? If you're managing a team, will you split the team in half and manage one half each or will you jointly manage everyone? Your immediate manager will be the decider on most of these questions, but remember that most managers don't have experience of managing job shares, so they'll need a settling in time too.

Ultimately, job sharing offers you the benefits of working part-time, but with the requirement to work very closely with someone else. The word 'share' is vital to bear in mind if you want to have a successful job share arrangement.

Despite all the options available for returning to work, many women feel that a full- or part-time job is no longer right for them. If this is the case, you may be considering taking some time out to be a full-time mum, which is the topic of the next chapter.

CHAPTER 4

Being a Full-time Mum

When a lot of women think about what to do after maternity leave they give themselves the two extreme choices of going back to work or becoming a full-time mum. I hope this book shows you that there are far more options (and combinations of options) than just these two, but, nevertheless, being a full-time mum is a valid choice and one which many women make, so let's look at what it's all about.

A good place to start is with the term I'm mainly using, 'full-time mum'. I know this isn't popular with some people. Personally, I dislike 'stay-at-home mum' which to me seems to describe mums by what they're *not* doing. It seems to imply that they're *not* out working, they're just 'staying at home'. Likewise, people have said to me that full-time mum seems a bit offensive to those who go to work full-time – does it make them 'part-time mums'? Of course, it doesn't. Once we're a mum, we're a mum 24/7 whether we're physically with our children or not. We could debate terminology all day, but the book would never have got written if I did! I decided I preferred to say full-time mums because they are usually replacing full-time work with their responsibilities as parents. They're still 'working' full-time in some sense, but it's the work of parenting (and usually housework too). It feels more technically accurate to me, but by all means use whatever term you feel comfortable with in your own conversations.

When I've spoken to women about what they fear most about being a full-time mum there is one thing which crops up over and above anything else. It's worded in different ways – sometimes the fear is about how society sees you, or about how your partner sees you, or your friends, or even how you see yourself – but it all boils down to one thing. These women fear becoming 'just a mum'.

Now we all know that we hold different identities depending on when and by whom we're observed. At work, you might be a police officer, or a teacher, or an architect. At home, you might be a sister, or a wife, or a daughter, or all of these things. But there's something about becoming a mum which makes us scared of losing some of our identity so that all we are is just 'Mum'.

These especially worries women who have worked hard to attain qualifications and then become successful in their career. They define themselves partly by the professional standing they've achieved, and so they should. No one gets to be a doctor or a lawyer by lazing around and doing no work, and those who have achieved career success should be proud of themselves.

But you don't have to be giving up (or putting on hold) a career as a doctor to be worried about people losing respect for you. People from all walks of life and all levels of career have the same fear. No matter how successful you've been or how far you've got, there's something about being paid to do your job which makes you feel that you have value in society.

Posts on the Internet implying that stay-at-home mums do nothing all day except lie around and nap, and perhaps change a nappy every so often, do nothing to support the reality that staying at home with your kids is hard work. But worse than that, they tend to imply that looking after your own kids is something that isn't a valuable contribution to society. And that's what hurts many full-time mums more than people believing they're not busy – people believing that mums are of no use to society unless they're working in a job.

It makes me angry that anyone should believe that their job or their worth is so much higher than anyone else's, but especially so when they are judging something they don't understand. I could go on for hours about how much hard work is involved in running a house and looking after kids full-time, as well as banging on about how much positive (or negative) impact you can have on tiny developing human beings through your daily words and actions. Your role as a parent is vital in guiding how your children develop and the kind of people they become, so choosing to devote yourself full-time to that role is anything but worthless to society.

But my anger won't help you make this decision. And getting angry about it yourself won't either. If you want to choose to be a full-time mum then you need to own your decision, because you may find yourself feeling like you have to justify and defend your choice. Over the years when I've had conversations with other mums about what they do for a living, the ones who are full-time mums often apologise for it.

Please don't ever feel you have to apologise for being a mum who stays home to look after your kids. In the same way a working mum should never have to apologise for putting her career first at times, you should never have to apologise for putting your family above all else, either for a short time or for many years.

COPING WITH KIDS FULL-TIME

Once you get past the identity issue and feel you could be comfortable in the role of full-time mum, the other major thing to consider is whether you can cope with the intensity of being home with your children full-time.

I'm going to be a bit controversial and say that I did not really enjoy being a full-time mum. Okay, it's fair to say that the time I found myself in that position, I'd just separated from my husband and moved 250 miles away from my established life. I had no money, no childcare and therefore no time to work on my freelance business. So there was more going on than just 'being a full-time mum', but even taking my personal stresses out of it, I still think I wouldn't be cut out for staying at home and caring for children full-time. Like with all jobs, some will love it and thrive and some will find it heavy going. It's worth spending the time when you're on maternity leave to assess whether this is something you really would want to do full-time when your leave comes to an end.

What did I find the most difficult elements? Well, firstly I'm a bit of a homebody. I don't want to go out every day because I generally enjoy being in my own home. But I couldn't really enforce that on my kids and keeping a 2- or 3-year-old cooped up inside all day is hard work. So the first thing I'd say about 'stay-at-home' mums is that they rarely stay at home. You'll probably find yourself out and about as much as possible, attending music groups, stay and plays, baby and toddler groups, ballet classes, etc. The activities on offer are endless and, while you don't have to go to everything, you'll probably feel it's best for your child if you take them to as many activities as you're comfortable with. Of course, if you love getting out and about and meeting up with other parents then this whole point is a definite positive and you can ignore my negativity about it. With hindsight I think I would have enjoyed many of these things more if I'd only had the one baby to look after.

Which leads to my second difficulty. I just wasn't comfortable in these kinds of activities. I struggled at local stay and play groups, because my twins made me 'different'. I never got a chance to talk to other mums because while they were able to focus their attention on keeping one child occupied or out of danger, my eyes were darting all over the room as I watched two toddlers stagger from place to place, occasionally snatching toys, as toddlers do, and never once playing together. One memorable music group, I looked round the room to see everyone else happily singing with their baby on their lap and a percussion instrument in one hand, while I had no spare hands and two wriggling babies hitting each other over the head with maracas. I hated every minute of it and never went back.

Which is why when I found a group where I felt understood and welcomed, it completely changed my whole outlook. At the twins group, everyone understood what it was like to go to a toddler session and spend the entire time in the toilet playing relay nappy changing. Straight away people were jumping in to look after one twin while I dealt with the other. The mix of ages – from newborn to five – really helped as there were older children playing independently which left their mums available to help others, something I was happily able to do when mine became one of the older sets. For two years that group was like a lifeline to me. I made new friends, some of whom I now count among my closest friends. Other people I know found great support from their NCT group, with parents they met at antenatal classes becoming lifelong friends, and always with a child almost exactly the same age.

A support network of friends and/or family is essential if you're going to be a full-time mum. There may be times when you feel isolated or different, or not up to the 'job' of parenting full-time, and you need people around you to talk to or even to babysit for a few hours. I've already said that I didn't necessarily like going out every day, but I had to make sure I did, not only to keep my kids happy, but also so I could speak to other adults which is so important when you spend all day caring for kids.

My final point about coping with kids full-time is being prepared with activities. When my kids were babies there was lots to do just to keep things running. Between changing and feeding and letting them roll or crawl around, the first year was mostly about the practical stuff. As they grew into toddlers and pre-schoolers I needed to be more prepared with activities like painting or drawing or making things. Perhaps I'm being hard on myself, but I'm not a natural crafter and I don't think I've been very good at that stuff. I feel it was at this point, more than when they were babies, that my lack of experience with kids in general really made a difference.

I think the bottom line here is that your personal support network, home environment, and how much you enjoy play and activities, can have a huge impact on how easy or hard you find it to cope with kids full-time. Don't be put off because I didn't like it, but equally if you do think it's something you might struggle with don't feel like you'd be the only one!

MAKE TIME FOR YOURSELF

Which brings me to another point. Make time for yourself

away from your kids. When you spend all day every day pushing a buggy or being trailed by small children, no matter how much you love them, you do feel like you need a break from them. So make sure you get one. Whether it's an evening out or an afternoon at home alone at the weekend while your partner takes over, make sure you get it. A vital element of retaining your identity is to do stuff you would normally do – whether it's an exercise class, going swimming or meeting up with friends. If you're doing stuff you'd have chosen to do before you became a mum, then you're maintaining that continuity despite being a mum now as well.

Once you've worked out which activities to do, built your support network, found new friends and left enough time for being a grown up, what else do you need to know about being a full-time mum?

YOUR RELATIONSHIP

Being a full-time mum might change the nature of your relationship with your husband or partner quite drastically. I'm going to assume that before you had children you and your partner both worked and you were probably reasonably familiar with the kind of work each other did. The thing about being a full-time mum is that it's unlikely your partner is going to understand all that it entails, so there are plenty of chances for misunderstandings and unrealistic expectations.

For instance, when my twins were around one, a typical

day might have seen us heading out at 11am, by the time breakfast and morning playing and napping had finished. Maybe we'd have lunch out and then get home mid-afternoon where there'd be more napping and playing and eating. Then there would be feeding and nappy changes, some of which were bound to involve mess and a change of clothing (for me or the baby, or both), and then the other change of clothing after eating, and then maybe some bathing too. Perhaps somewhere in the middle of all that I'd find the time to throw some clothes in the washing machine and set it going. If I was really lucky I may even have had time to hang up the clothes to dry at some point within a few hours of the wash finishing or to pick up a few toys and put them away. If my husband had come home then and wondered where his dinner was, I might have exploded.

Just because you've been literally in the house doesn't necessarily mean that you should be in charge of every domestic thing that happens in that house. Domestic chores can still be done in the evening as they would have had to be done when you both worked full-time. I think it's fair that some tasks can be part of your day since you're home and able to do them, but I think it's unfair for anyone to assume that looking after kids is not the same as a full-time job and therefore can just be dropped at any moment in order to do the washing up. In reality, when my kids were one my husband was a full-time dad and I worked full-time, getting home at around 6.30pm on a good day. I didn't expect dinner made every night and nor did I get it. I understood what hard work it was and that some days feel like they fly past in a rush and yet you have nothing to show for it. But that doesn't mean you did nothing.

Your partner may be mentally tired after commuting to work and being in an office all day. You may be mentally and physically drained from looking after a small child all day. Who makes the dinner is anyone's guess. You shouldn't assume that you've had it hardest because you've had no adult company for three days and he shouldn't assume that you could have done all the cooking, cleaning and phoned the gas company, since you're at home all day anyway.

These are the kinds of things which fester away beneath the surface and cause huge resentment and rifts between couples. Don't let that happen. If you decide to become a full-time mum, discuss these things with your partner. Decide on which chores and jobs are priorities and which should be left if you're both tired. Decide who will do what (and when) based on your strengths and the practicalities of your lifestyle. Being a parent is hard work, especially if, as for many of us, you don't have lots of family around to help out.

In most cases choosing to become a full-time mum while your partner continues to work means that he is earning the money and you're 'living off him' now. This can be pretty hard for many of us women to get used to, having been brought up our whole lives to believe that we're capable of surviving without a man. This requires a major mindset shift. If you're staying home to look after the baby and your partner is working, that is a partnership in the same way that if you ran a business, one person might do sales and the other accounts. A family is a partnership. If it falls to one member of that family to look after children while the other earns money that doesn't make either 'job' more important or worthwhile than the other. If you weren't there to look after the kids, then your husband couldn't work as he does, and vice versa.

Supporting your family is one job split into two halves. One person supports financially and the other practically. Or a combination of that. It's important that when you decide to stay at home to look after your kids your partner understands his role in the family. He is not the breadwinner looking after his wife and child. You are both looking after the child but he's doing the money thing and you're doing the daily caring thing. That is a partnership and it means you both support each other in your roles.

Being a full-time mum can be a wonderful experience and I fear I've painted a pretty dull picture of it by addressing the difficulties you might face, but that's only because you'll need to deal with those things in order to enjoy a positive experience. Being able to be at home with your child every day is special and important. And I don't say that flippantly. The benefits to your child's happiness, behaviour, and development from being at home with you rather than spending long hours in nursery have been proven in various studies. We all do the best we can for our children, and sometimes childcare is necessary, but don't underestimate or downplay what a gift to your children it is to put them before your career and choose to raise them full-time. And it's not all sacrifice either. I know I've made a big thing of building your support network and taking time out as if it's one hard slog. Some days it does feel like it is, but the rewards are there daily too – like being there for all the milestones instead of hearing about them from a childminder or nursery staff.

I suppose I could liken it to training for a huge sporting event, like the Olympics. It's hard work, and there are days when it won't all come together and you'll doubt yourself and feel you're not good enough. But it's totally worth it for the day when it does come together and you find yourself on top of your game. And that's kind of what full-time mumming is like. It's mostly hard work, made even harder by the fact that no one can see just how much work you're putting in to it, but the rewards make it so worthwhile.

It's only a shame they don't hand out gold medals for it.

CHAPTER 5

Self-employment

Starting a business is not for the faint-hearted, but, that said, it also doesn't have to be the big scary thing that only 'other people' do. Early on in my self-employment journey I heard someone say that it's the biggest self-development course you could ever take. I've heard similar versions of that statement many times since, because it's absolutely true.

Nothing brings you face-to-face with your fears, strengths, weaknesses, mental blocks and self-belief in the way that starting your own business does. For some that might be a reason to avoid it like the plague; for others it will be a reason to rush headlong into it. As with all the options discussed in this book, the choice is yours. This is certainly not the easy option, but then none of the options are easy.

There are, of course, things that make it easier or harder. For instance, if your pre-baby income was the second household income and was only really needed to pay for luxuries, or you have income from a rental property or plenty of savings, then the stress of starting a business will be much less than for a woman who was previously the breadwinner and has no savings. In that case giving up your income to start a business will change the family earning dynamic considerably and will put a lot of pressure on you to start making a profit from day one. I would argue, however, that the overall process will be quite similar. The blocks and rewards ahead will be significant whether you're relying on your new business income in order to feed your kids or for a bit of extra cash for an exotic family holiday. Having money behind you when you start out might be helpful as it takes away that pressure to perform right away, but it's very easy to waste your money on courses, advice and systems you don't need, or get complacent and spend too much upfront on infrastructure and expenses before you've proved your business model is working. For this reason, I'm leaving the money talk for a bit later in the chapter.

In the meantime, I want to look in more depth at the idea of the business model. Put simply, a business model is what your business does and how it makes money. It may seem obvious to explain that, but many people don't think through this basic foundation before they start and then get overwhelmed trying to squeeze too many different facets into their own new business.

I've made no secret of the fact that my own business ventures haven't all been successful. But don't take my lack of success as an indicator that the advice in this section might be rubbish. One of the joys of trying and failing and trying again is that you try a lot of stuff. This means I have first-hand experience of most of the different business models I'm going to cover. Also included are tips and advice I've learnt from those who have been successful – women I interviewed on the Maternity Leavers podcast or worked with in some other way. In any case, the point of this book is not to teach you how to start a business, it is to help you decide whether starting a business is the correct route for you on your next career step and, if so, how to get started on that journey.

As I said at the beginning of the book, every person reading this book will have a different skillset and work experience behind them, and likewise you all have a different path ahead of you. And so it goes for starting a business. There are so many different businesses in different industries that are all doing different things in order to stand out and find their clients and customers. All I can do here is guide you towards some foundations for a business model which suits your skills and lifestyle. After that it's up to you.

It's important to bear in mind that this isn't a 'business book' and my selection of business models isn't any kind of classic business models list. It's basically just a rundown of the types of businesses you could get involved in. When you think about 'starting a business' you probably already have an idea in your head about how 'a business' looks, so I want to expand on that idea and raise a few more options you may not have considered.

CASE STUDY

> *Her story*
>
> Once I went on maternity leave with my eldest son, I realised there was no way I wanted to go back to be working for someone else if I didn't have to. I started my own business while on maternity leave, launched my own iPhone app and then started working hard to pave the way for quitting my job. By the time I returned to work from my second maternity leave, it was as if I didn't exist at work. I'd gone from being one of the most senior people in the organisation to being stuck at a desk in the attic with nothing to do. I worked as hard as I could on my own business and left four months after returning from maternity leave. My business now employs eight people and has sold products in 96 countries. We have thousands of customers. Not a day goes by that I am not relieved to have set up for myself!
>
> Lorraine Dallmeier, www.formulabotanica.com

SOLOPRENEURS AND FREELANCING

If you've spent any time at all poking around on the Internet at business coaches or websites about starting your own business, you've no doubt also been bombarded by Facebook ads about rags-to-riches tales of people down to their last penny and now raking in six figures from a laptop on the beach. Some of these people may be telling the truth. Many aren't. But, either way, this is the perception of the 'Internet solopreneur'.

I'm not even sure that 'solopreneur' is a proper word, but it's one used commonly in the online business community. A few years ago, we'd have called people like these freelancers. But the thing about freelancers is that they only offer their service. The Internet has allowed many who would have been traditional freelancers to build a business around their skills by easily being able to offer and sell digital packages of their expertise. In this way, solopreneurs are able to make money from traditional freelance work – the service element of their business – and supplement it with income from digital products. Some have managed to flip this round so that most of their money comes from digital products with little, if any, coming from service-based work.

What characterises the business of a solopreneur is that the business is them and they are the business. There are no employees. When there is enough work and money coming into the business, the solopreneur will probably take on a virtual assistant (VA) and perhaps freelancers to do things like Facebook ads, product launch marketing or social media management. So, they build a team around them, but don't take on staff in the traditional sense.

The 'product' being sold is the expertise of the solopreneur themselves, whatever that may be. For instance, a business coach will be selling their expertise on marketing, building a business and setting up processes and systems, while a copywriter would be selling their expertise on writing headlines that hook readers in or campaigns which tug at people's emotions.

The actual products they sell might be online courses, workbooks, eBooks and paperback books, audio recordings, webinars or video training. Some may be tangible real-life products, but most will be digital. You're buying the information rather than 'a thing'. Some of the products will be free (like an eBook of top 10 marketing tips) to entice you in to their 'sales funnel'. Once they have your email address you'll then get emails inviting you to buy increasingly advanced and in-depth products (like an eight-week e-course) as your own knowledge and expertise grows and you want to learn more. Some solopreneurs also have services like one-to-one mentoring, coaching or advice sessions, or they may offer a 'done for you' service, such as managing your marketing or social media, or writing your website copy.

If you have some kind of expertise and you're happy and motivated to work alone on your business – at least until you get to the point where your business warrants hiring freelancers – this could be a good model for you. Think of expertise you have from your previous jobs, qualifications or even hobbies and interests: health, nutrition, exercise, personal training, yoga, Pilates, technology, copywriting, photography, tarot reading and hypnotherapy have all been the basis for businesses. If you're a really good organiser and have some office work experience, you could become a VA and get hired by other solopreneurs. To some extent, any expertise will do. What matters is that you can turn what you know into a service which you do for people or a product where people can learn to do it themselves.

The question of product versus service and the idea of passive income comes up a lot when you hang out in this space so it's worth thinking about your own views on it. The laptop on the beach advertisers all have the same basic message – stop exchanging time for money. In other words, don't spend your time freelancing because there's a finite amount of time you can spend on service-based work and therefore only a finite amount of money you can earn from it. Instead, make more digital products and your earnings are never capped.

My own views are that, in general, services are more valuable to the customer, especially when they are a busy solopreneur or business owner themselves. When someone wants copywriting done, for instance, they want it done. They don't want to sign up for an eight-week home study course on how to write good copy. However, digital products are more valuable to you as a business owner because you can make them once and sell them over and over again. This is the holy grail of passive income that online marketers rave about. Produce an online course and all you have to do is sell it. This idea is especially desirable to mums who are not afraid of hard work, who already have 24 hours' worth of work a day in the shape of a baby and are looking for ways to earn money in a way that works alongside this.

However, selling an e-course is a full-on job by itself. Unless you're already pretty famous, creating an online course from your own expertise is the easy bit; building an audience for it is much more time-consuming. If you know your subject and put in the time to make the course really good, then you've created a really valuable product and you should be very proud of yourself. But even fantastic courses don't sell themselves. Marketing that product will require creating and maintaining a website, attracting leads, collecting email addresses, writing emails, writing blog posts, being present on social media and perhaps making videos or podcasts too. None of these are tiny jobs.

I don't say any of this to put you off. In fact, most of these tasks are fun and many people get into the world of online business because they would rather spend their time making videos or writing blog posts than attending video conferences or creating yet another dull PowerPoint presentation. I say it to be realistic about the difference between 'passive' income and that which you might charge by the hour or project. Yes, exchanging time for money might get a bad rap from the online 'package up your expertise' community, but it's easier to sell and may actually take up less time in the long run.

My point is to make sure you don't rule out charging for a service in favour of creating an online course because you think the income will be more passive and easy to fit around nap times. In my experience, there isn't much difference between the two until you've built up a massive following and people scramble to buy everything you put out for sale.

For the record, I also disagree with charging an hourly rate if your service is something like consulting or copywriting. Charging per project (for example, pay X amount and get X result) is far better and avoids you having to account for your every move to a client. With a flat rate agreed up front, it also makes it easier to request that your client pays you 50 per cent in advance of the job starting, which is standard in many industries and also great for your cash flow. Just make sure that if you offer a flat rate, you're absolutely sure that it covers all the time and expenses that the project requires otherwise you may end up working long hours to finish a project that you didn't charge enough for.

The trick, whichever option you choose, is to be very clear about which tasks need to be done in order to actually earn money. It's so easy in this kind of business to pour time and energy into 'getting known' and then find out that it's had little to no impact on your actual income. Keep a keen eye on what activities are bringing you real business and squeeze as many of those as you can into those precious nap times!

A final point I want to make is about making sure you

spend time with 'real people'. The Internet makes it very easy to build a business where you never see or speak to your clients, and if you do it's likely to be over the phone or Skype. If you're splitting your time between parenting and working on an Internet based business it can feel pretty lonely and isolating. So please make sure you get out and about, either as part of your work (e.g. networking meetings or co-working spaces) or to see friends and family socially.

DIRECT SALES

Direct sales are also known as multi-level marketing (MLM), network marketing or party plans. There are hundreds of companies which sell their products through local agents who may be known as ambassadors, consultants, stylists or representatives. The way it works is that you have your own business but you sell products from the parent company and earn commission from the sales. The traditional method of selling is through home parties, where you find hosts to invite their friends round to their house and you run a 'party' introducing and demonstrating the product. As many of the companies sell beauty products, you can usually bill it as a pamper party where people will enjoy using the products whether they buy anything or not, but of course the aim of the party from the consultant's point of view is to sell as many products as possible. Usually the host gets incentives and free products based on how much their friends buy too.

You'll usually get your own website, which is branded and looks the same as all the other consultants', but if people buy from your direct link, you get the commission. For years mainly women have been doing direct sales jobs alongside full-time work or parenting. Years ago the options might have been limited to Avon, Ann Summers or Tupperware, but now there are hundreds of options, all with varying compensation plans and benefits. A modern development is the rise of the Facebook party where the consultant runs a series of giveaways and games and people attend via their computer or phone – ideal for a new mum who wants to become a consultant but finds it hard to get out in the evenings.

Some plans are very simple – you buy catalogues from the company, perhaps some stock too, share them with your friends and customers whenever you see them or at a home party, or hire a stall at an event, and place orders which you then distribute to your customers. What makes a direct selling company into an MLM is when you are able to recruit team members too. That's what can make this otherwise relatively low earning potential into something much bigger. When you have a team, or 'downline', below you, you also get a cut of commission on the products they sell, as well as what you sell yourself. And so it goes on down through the line with potentially each member of one person's team also having a team of their own. Of course, the commission structure doesn't go down forever – it's usually two or three levels deep – although if you have a team below you of hundreds or thousands, which is quite feasible because of the way the structures work, you could be making a lot of money.

Before you get too excited though, it's worth a bit of a reality check on MLM. It all sounds pretty easy, but those who make a lot of money from it are definitely in the minority of the total number of those who sign up. Many join companies, lured by the low cost of entry. Most 'starter packs', which are your 'business in a box' (a mixture of product samples, free stuff for you and marketing materials like catalogues and flyers) are usually sold for less than £100 and the kit in them is clearly worth more than that. So, lots of people sign up with only the intention of getting the free or discounted stuff and maybe selling enough of it to get their money back. Others fling themselves into the business, bombarding their family and friends and social media feeds with details of their products and trying to sell it at every opportunity they get. And once they work out that the only way to make a living from it is to recruit a team, they also end up bombarding their friends with their fantastic and lucrative 'business opportunity'. When that doesn't work, they move into local selling groups on Facebook where, in some of them, you're far more likely to find a post about joining the team of a direct sales rep than you are to ever find anything to buy.

This is why direct sales has a bad reputation in the business community. That said, it's the actions of many direct sellers that is the problem, not the opportunity itself. In the hands of the right person, a direct sales business can be highly lucrative and lots of fun. It's not really for me to say who the 'right person' is, but they need to be able to sell without coming across like a used car salesman, build a rapport with everyone they meet and be able to drop details of the product and business opportunity into a conversation, again without coming across as desperate or insincere. Most people who are in an MLM company truly believe that their business opportunity is good for the person they mention it to, but many struggle with how to discuss it naturally.

MY EXPERIENCE

I could use myself as a case study here as I'm a consultant in a direct sales company called Jamberry which sells nail wraps and other nail care items. I wear virtually no make-up and find it hard to stick to even a basic skincare regime, so I've never been interested in the companies that sell beauty products. No matter how good their product is, I figured I couldn't sell something I wouldn't spend my own money on. But nail wraps, yes, I could totally sell that because I loved them the minute I tried them. (If you've never heard of them, they're pieces of thin vinyl which stick to your natural nails, allowing you to apply detailed nail art at home without the time and expense of going to a professional nail art salon.) When I discovered them at a local May Day fete, the woman demonstrating them had only signed up herself the week before. To cut a long story short, I went to her launch party a few days later and signed up there and then.

Now, this story gets interesting because, while I immediately loved the product and still do five months later, I've not made my business into the high-earning success story I hoped it would be. While I've found it pretty easy to find customers and sell the product, I haven't taken on any recruits. I've wanted to, but either haven't got into conversations with the right people or I haven't 'sold' the opportunity well enough to the people I have spoken to. Which means that, although I easily made back my initial outlay (pretty much entirely at my own launch party) and even covered most of the costs of other things like business cards and a bag for all my kit (the kind of things which are not necessary but you're likely to want to invest in), it never transformed into the 'full-time income' I hoped it would. That said, there are plenty of people around me, in my upline and on my level, who are doing really well in their own businesses, selling hundreds of pounds worth of stock every month and taking on a new recruit every few weeks.

Some things about direct sales really appeal to me, like being part of a team which is something you just don't get with solopreneurism. Even if you hire a VA or other freelance staff, they don't care about your business as much as you do, whereas in MLM you're all looking for ways to market the same products. Sharing is common and there's a proper team atmosphere. Team managers offer incentives to their teams and there's a culture of sharing, supporting and helping. Let's face it, my upline benefits from every sale or recruit that I bring in, so support and advice are not hard to come by. And I genuinely don't mean this in a cynical way. The truth is that the whole team benefits from what the whole team achieves, just like in any team game, so while there's an element of offering help in order to help yourself, it's still a supportive community to be part of and one you wouldn't get from any other self-employed venture.

Yet despite all this camaraderie, there's a distinct down side to having so many consultants: saturation of the market. When Jamberry launched, several people in my local area signed up to be consultants, and it felt like every time I mentioned the product to someone they were either fed up of hearing about it or they already had a consultant they were ordering through. Perhaps this was just the hype of the launch and it'll settle down, but I think it's true to say that when a product or company becomes popular and has a lot of established consultants, it can sometimes be hard to establish a customer base in your area without treading on someone else's toes. It's not impossible, but it does take hard work and smart thinking to overcome.

From the minute I signed up there were plenty of helpful resources available to me. At first I read, watched and followed all the training, advice and stories. But I still wasn't getting any recruits and my sales after the first couple of months were below average. I enjoy talking about nails and going to parties where I demonstrate the product, meet new people and chat about nail wraps. But when it comes to 'closing the deal', I only feel comfortable placing orders when people have decided by themselves what they want with no input from me. I also don't feel comfortable approaching or chatting to people about 'the opportunity'. So, from a sales and recruiting perspective, I'm not that good at either. The more I realise I'm not a salesperson, the more withdrawn I get from my business. I still place orders for myself and any of my friends and customers who ask me to, but I'm no longer looking for sales or party bookings. It's all become very passive.

I think this is what happens to other people who join MLMs or direct sales too. They may be successful at first because they're offering a new product to new people, whether those people are friends or strangers, but after an initial success (or in some cases, not even much of an initial success), they become a bit disillusioned and then just step back and 'give up'. And this is what has happened with me. On the one hand, I was hoping that a light-hearted nail wrap business was just what I needed and I thought I could make a huge success of it, but on the other hand it now doesn't feel very 'me'. That said, it is as much about the effort I put in as it is my own attitude to giving up and moving on. Direct sales does make a good side business but it requires time and commitment. My heart and head moved on to other things and I found I didn't have time to keep up the momentum needed to keep the business going. The low cost of entry worked against me because once I'd made my money back I didn't feel bad about letting it slide in favour of other projects.

However, despite Jamberry not working out for me as a lucrative business, it certainly gave me some good experiences. When I started, I was bold enough to go up to mums in the playground I didn't really know that well and invite them to my launch party. I made quite a few new friends that way, which was brilliant. I also met people at parties and generally socialised more, which is a good thing for most new mums to try. Running parties gave me confidence and my nails still look fabulous every day. I don't want my story to be unhelpful or off-putting. There are plenty of success stories out there and if you're someone who naturally loves sales and meeting people then you could absolutely make a success of a direct sales business if you find a product that suits you. What I wanted was to share how easy it is to lose interest in this kind of business. Some might call it failure, but I prefer not to as it's just one of many experiences I've had. I also didn't lose anything and I've still got a business I can resurrect at any time if I feel I want to.

Finally, I want to put aside any worries you may have about scams and pyramid schemes which often get associated with these kinds of businesses – there's nothing dodgy about direct sales with an established company selling tangible products. As with all careers, it will suit some people and not others, which means some will be successful while others will not. I want to finish with an inspiring story from someone who has made it work really well for themselves.

CASE STUDY

Her story

My name is Rachel Chan and I am 25 years old. When I fell pregnant at 22, not long after graduating from university and settling into my corporate account management career, I feared for what my prospects were once my maternity leave was over. My initial thoughts were that I would go back to work after a year off and have to get family members / childcare / nursery to help with the care of the baby. But that all changed when my daughter was born. Unexpectedly she arrived five weeks early and as soon as she was born we were rushed to Yorkhill Children's Hospital where we were informed that she would have to undergo major surgery to fix a blockage in her bowel. At that point my world was completely turned upside down and all that was important to me was the recovery of our baby. We spent the first two months of her life in intensive care at Yorkhill Hospital, while she recovered from her operation. As a new mum this was an extremely challenging time, not being able to hold my baby or have quality alone time and I was so worried about whether she would even know who I was. (It's crazy when I say this, knowing the strong bond we have now.) Fast forward three years and I'm pleased to say she made a full recovery and is a very happy, healthy little girl and has just started preschool this week! Once we got home from hospital and after taking some time off to spend with my daughter, in January 2014 I set up a home-based online health, beauty and wellness business. My goal was to build up my business to enable me to give up my full-time job. Within six months I had matched my full-time income working part-time around my family commitments, often taking my daughter along with me to coffee meetings to share my new business with people. By July 2014, my pay cheque had overtaken what I was earning in my previous 9 to 5 job and this happened to also be the month I had my back-to-work interview to discuss a plan for my return to work. I made the decision not to go back to full-time employment and entered the world of being fully self-employed, and I have never looked back.

I love the freedom and flexibility of being my own boss and getting to decide my own schedule. It hasn't come without its challenges of juggling work life and family life: often I was working with my baby on my lap, which sometimes was so amazing and other times not so much! But I would not trade it for the world and I am so grateful that I've been able to be a stay-at-home mum while still having a career and building a business that's supporting my family and me. My daughter has just turned three and I've been able to be a part of all those special moments that as a new parent you don't want to miss out on. I felt like I had missed out on so much with her having a difficult start to life, so this was absolutely the catalyst for me to go out and do something different in order to be able to be fully present in my daughter's life. She has been my 'why' and the driver behind my success in my business. Now with baby number two on the way and a successful global online business, I'm excited to do it all again, but this time with a toddler in tow as well! Has it been easy? Absolutely not. Has it been worth it? One hundred per cent YES!

Rachel Chan, Limitless Living, Arbonne

NG AND LICENSING

Franchising

In the same vein as direct sales, franchising offers you the chance to buy a ready-made business. The company's branding and processes are already established and you buy the right to be the only business of your type in a particular region or post code area. Kids' activity franchises are popular with mums, where they run a local business offering, say, drama classes, but branded with a national name that potential customers may already be familiar with. A big difference to direct sales is this ability to 'own' a geographical area which means you won't have others around you selling exactly the same brand and product.

Franchise companies often sell services or classes, like cleaning or driving lessons, but they can be physical shops too, with two of the best known franchises being McDonald's and Subway. All of these stores have owner/managers who have bought into the franchise, so they've bought the right to use the branding and the processes, but it's up to them to buy the actual stock or rent their premises out of their own business. If you bought a kids' activity franchise you would mainly be buying training to enable you to teach the classes in the company's specific way, and you would benefit from the national advertising and brand awareness, but it would be up to you as a small local business owner to advertise and fill your classes. Franchises usually have strict rules and standards which you would need to stick to. So if you bought a franchise teaching kids drama classes, for instance, you would need to teach them the way they train you to and use the materials and songs that they provide you with.

On the one hand this is brilliant if you want to get on and run classes without having to design and prepare all the materials and concepts yourself from scratch, but on the other hand, you will need time to get yourself familiar with all the processes, methods and materials you will be using. On top of that you'll need to establish your customer base and launch your business as you would any other.

Franchises tend to cost several thousand pounds, sometimes with ongoing monthly fees on top, so they are a significant investment and not something like direct sales or freelancing that you can try out, tweak, yet easily walk away from if it's not working out. But this also means the chance of success is higher. You're buying a business that has already been tested and trialled in other areas and the psychological push to make it work is far stronger due to the amount you've invested. There are usually other franchisees that you can speak to and share ideas with, and the franchise owner themselves will be supporting you and sharing their advice and experience about growing your business. It's in their interest for their franchisees to be successful as it all reflects on them as a company, as does everything you do, as well as the fact that they generally (but not always) require a cut of your profits.

Although a franchisee is self-employed, they're a bit like an employee in some ways, but still far more autonomous than when in actual employment. The best analogy would be to think of it as an independent branch of a company, so your 'head office' still retains control, might inspect or observe you, and might take a cut of the profits, but the day-to-day running is entirely your responsibility and your salary depends on how well your branch performs.

Licencing

A licence is similar to a franchise but less comprehensive. Licences allow you to license the intellectual property (IP) of the main company but they don't retain so much control over how you use it. If you buy a licence (which is usually in the hundreds rather than thousands) you are buying the right to use the company's branding and material, but they are not usually obliged to ensure that you have no nearby competitors, for instance, and they wouldn't request any cut of your profits. And while they may provide some training, it is unlikely to be as in-depth and comprehensive as that of a franchise, focusing only on the material you're licensing and not on how to run a business using it.

A well-known company which licenses out its brand is Disney. Many manufacturing companies buy licences to put the Disney branding on their products. A smaller example is BabyNatal who run antenatal and other baby related classes, and who offer a licence to become one of their teachers.

You'll find franchising and licensing opportunities on job

websites. Many aimed at mums have dedicated sections for these self-employed 'jobs' alongside their traditional employed job sections.

Do your research

I can't stress enough that when it comes to any of these types of opportunities, you should do your research, especially where the cost of entry is high or where there are ongoing costs. You want to be sure that you can be fully committed to selling the product or teaching the classes in the way that you are meant to and that you can comply with the standards and processes that the company demands – this especially means taking into account your childcare and family situation.

Read the contract with a fine-tooth comb. Ask a lawyer to read over it too if you can. You need to know exactly how much money you'll be paying and when. For instance, many licences need to be renewed annually unless you give notice to cancel and some may provide materials on loan for demonstration purposes. If you just let your business lapse and don't give appropriate notice or return materials, then you continue to be liable for your annual fees. While it may feel a bit like planning a divorce before you get married, it's always smart to read contracts and know exactly what you're getting yourself into.

It would also be highly advisable to speak at length to a current or previous franchisee in the company you want to join, preferably several of them. As I keep saying, you learn just as much from people that have failed as those who are successful, so don't just speak to the featured, ubersuccessful franchisee who the company has plastered all over their marketing materials. Seek out the ones who have tried and failed, or who are finding it tough going. You don't want to be put off by others' negativity but you do want to be pragmatic and to see things from a realistic perspective. You want to know why they're finding it tough; perhaps in practice the hours required are longer than the company estimates or maybe what is working fine in an urban area is proving heavy going for a franchisee in a rural area. People come up with all sorts of reasons for failing and some are just excuses, so watch out for anyone who doesn't take on any of the responsibility themselves. The truth is that many people fail because they didn't put the work in, but it can be very useful to learn what obstacles they faced so you can work out if the same obstacles might trip you up.

Research is important but there's always a risk of over researching things, especially on the Internet where it's simple to just click through from one site to another blog to another report of how past franchisees or licensees have fared. By all means start there, but it's far more important to speak to people and ask questions rather than just taking what they've written at face value. Like all parts of your research, if you find someone who failed at it, take it as input but don't base your whole decision on one person's poor experience.

And finally, are you willing to comply with the procedures,

standards and methods? For instance, it would be no good buying a McDonald's franchise if you had strong vegan views. Okay, if your views were that strong I'd hope you wouldn't even consider it, but even minor changes or rebellions are not generally welcome within a franchise. That's not to say that companies won't consider suggestions from their franchisees, of course they should, but don't buy a franchise if you know you fundamentally disagree with an element of the method or if you're thinking of new and different ways of doing things before you even sign the contract. When you buy a franchise you're buying a well-established business process and brand. Switching it around or thinking you could do it better in a different way is not really in the spirit of franchising and you may end up disappointed or frustrated.

The biggest pro to franchising and licensing is having it all done for you. You're buying into a system or product that other people have made work, and your branding and national brand awareness is taken care of by head office. In effect, you've got a running start instead of a standing start like a solopreneur. But this doesn't guarantee success – only your hard work and dedication will do that.

RETAIL AND SELLING PRODUCTS

In the previous sections I looked mainly at service businesses or those where the products were informational or intangible. But there has always been trading of goods, so one business model you may want to consider is running a shop. I'm going to gloss over physical shops for the purposes of this book (only because if you're reading this you're probably looking for a more flexible way of working around your family and a physical shop is not likely to offer you that). So, I'll mostly be talking about online shops, but a lot of the advice is transferable.

There are really two big decisions to make if you think your future career lies in selling physical products:

1. What are you going to sell? Things you make or things made by other people? Are you going to use your love of knitting, sewing, crafting, baking, art or chutney-making to produce wonderful home-made gifts, or are you going to run a shop which sells third-party items, bought either from a wholesaler or other home-making businesses?
2. Are you going to build your own dedicated e-commerce website (or get it built for you) or are you going to use a third-party selling site like Etsy, Amazon or Society6? This third-party option could also include selling your items to an already established real world shop. The principles are similar – you're the supplier rather than the seller.

What are you going to sell?
If you're looking at home-made items, what are they? Are you particularly skilled at knitting or making clothes? Do you

have a hobby or previous career experience that means you're capable of making physical items that people want to buy? If so, great!

Now let's get real and practical. Many have gone before you to make beautiful things that just couldn't achieve the income that they wanted to make. In this more than in any other kind of business, it's worth doing a quick calculation before you even start daydreaming. Let's say your skill is crocheting monkeys. Cool. Who doesn't want a crocheted monkey? So, your monkeys look great. Each one takes a couple of hours to make and people are chomping at the bit to buy them for £10 each. Say you really want to earn £500 a month to contribute to the family pot – that's not even a full-time income, but just say it's your target for now – that's 50 monkeys. Which is 100 hours of work. Or 25 hours a week straightforward crocheting. That doesn't even include the cost of materials, any marketing of your monkeys or looking after your baby, etc. At a very basic level, it also means you're working for less than £5 an hour.

This is a pessimistic example but hardly extreme and I'm honestly not trying to put you off, but many craft items don't fetch a high sale price and will often take more than a couple of hours' work too. When you put the numbers down in the cold, hard light of day and scale them up to assess whether you have a realistic and sustainable income, you can see that it's difficult to make more than a very modest side-line income from a lot of home-made stuff. Which is fine if you enjoy it and just want an extra bit of income here and there, and if you don't want to shoot yourself after crocheting 100 monkeys in a month.

The fundamental principle of what I'm trying to highlight here is that when you're in the business of making stuff, you are limited by how much you can physically make. And it hardly needs saying that when you're caring for children, the demands on your time are so much higher than they were before you had kids. Crocheting a couple of monkeys in an evening may have been something you once enjoyed to wind down from the stress of your office job, but it may seem like an insurmountable task when you got no sleep last night and have been running round all day nappy changing, feeding, cleaning, nappy changing, feeding … and on and on. Don't make life difficult for yourself – if you're looking to leave a stressful traditional job, don't make your business more tiring and more time-consuming than your existing job is.

Above all, don't start if you're going to fall out of love with your passion. If you love knitting now, try forcing yourself to do more than you normally would in a day and do it to a deadline. Do that for a few days. Think of it like a business. Now, do you still love it? If yes then great, but if you find yourself hankering for the good old days when you looked forward to picking up your needles, yet after a few days of intensive work you want to poke them in your eyes, perhaps a knitting business isn't right for you. Not all passions are meant to turn into proper businesses. There's nothing to stop you doing it as a side business when and if you have the time and inclination to do it, but if you're looking to replace a full-time income and you can't or won't want to physically make the amount of stock you need to achieve that aim, then try another idea instead.

If you're still set on making stuff, and great if you are, consider options, such as getting freelancers to produce part or all of your products; buying elements ready-made so you just have to assemble them; or picking items that don't take much time to make in the first place or that can fetch a high price.

Handmade items can be big business and totally viable so don't be put off by my doom and gloom. In fact, if you find yourself being defensive and thinking of ways that your situation is different to the bleak one I painted, then good for you. There are plenty of artisans out there making a living and some making a killing. I just want you to be realistic about your products and your pricing. If you're amazing at carving wood, for instance, or pottery, then by all means go for the upmarket crowd and craft handmade items that costs hundreds or thousands. If you're producing stuff that is in demand and beautiful, then don't undercharge for it. Take into account your time, the cost of materials and the cost to sell (for example, marketing, advertising, time spent stood at a trade stall, etc.) and adjust your prices accordingly.

One other little point about handmade items – if your particular skill is baking or cooking, please find out the business implications of selling cakes, chutneys or other edible items.

You may need a food hygiene certificate, your kitchen may need to be inspected and there may be other rules and regulations. Again, I don't say this to put you off, but running a food business is necessarily more complicated, expensive and time-consuming than selling crocheted monkeys.

The other retail option is selling stuff made by other people and this may be ideal for you if you're more of a curator than a creator. If you have experience in the retail or buying sector then that's a bonus, but at the very basic level you need a shopfront – online most probably – and you need to buy the items you want to stock in your shop. Here, again, there are choices. You could buy manufactured items from wholesalers or you could go out and find handmade products that you want to sell and negotiate a deal with the maker to stock their product in your shop.

When looking at products and deciding on the branding and ethos of your shop, take into account what your motivation is. Do you want to curate and sell a certain type of product for the love of it or are you looking for products on which you can get the best margin? Are you looking to be a farm shop selling hand-chosen high quality local ingredients or a supermarket selling a big range of varying quality at low prices? Neither is the 'right' answer, but the way you run the business and deal with your suppliers – and particularly where you find your suppliers – will be different depending on which angle you're going for. Either way, you also have to look at the business side of things and make sure the numbers add up to profit.

How are you going to sell?

Which leads on to the next big decision of how you're going to sell your products. Do you want your own branded business or do you want the convenience of a third-party selling site? Your products will influence the method of sale and vice versa – they're not separate stand-alone decisions, but you have to start somewhere.

Third-party sites like Etsy already sell loads of handmade items and have a search function and a large number of customers – ideal if you're going down the handmade route. Of course, you still have to lure those customers to your little corner by using good product photography, great product descriptions and keywords, but essentially you're already inside a market where people come looking for the kind of stuff you're selling.

Other third-party options are eBay and Amazon. Not so great for the handmade stuff, although you do see things like that on there, but lots of people make their own stores on these platforms to sell products they buy wholesale. If you've ever bought from Amazon you'll see that sometimes the seller is a third party. When that's the case, sometimes the seller is informed of the order and they post it directly to the customer and other times the order is fulfilled and sent by Amazon using stock delivered to them directly by your manufacturer or wholesaler. So, you could run a business selling stock on Amazon without ever seeing the stock yourself.

An option if you're an artist or photographer is to sell your art through sites like Society6. On sites like these you create artwork – be it a drawing or a photo or lettering – and you upload it to the site as a high-resolution digital file. They then sell different products with your image on them and send you a cut of the sale price. So, you could design T-shirts or mugs or wall canvasses – the possibilities and products available are huge. Like Etsy, the customers are on the site because they're looking for products by independent artists, say an unusual iPhone case, so you need to label your work so that it appears in their searches. Beyond that, it's an easy way of getting your work out there and available for sale for a minimal outlay.

On the other hand, if you choose to run your own website, then you still need all the photography and descriptions but keywords become even more important because you're trying to catch people from all over the Internet. On top of those things you also need to come up with a company name and branding, and build your site. With a bit of technical knowledge and confidence you could set up an e-commerce site within WordPress and sell direct from there, but you'll most likely want to hire a web developer to build your website, and possibly a web designer too. I'll make no bones about it, this is a big job and will require upfront investment in a way that selling on Etsy won't. In fact, many start on Etsy to test the market, see how their product is received and build a loyal customer base, then break off into their own site when their brand is already quite well established. This is a really good strategy if you've just had a baby and want to grow your business gradually over several years as they grow older, and then make the larger investments of time and money when they start preschool or school.

Like with the other options we have explored, the platforms are out there and most are easy and cheap to access. The Internet makes it easy but you can also go local and sell items at fairs and events, or approach shops about stocking your wares. Whatever you want to sell there's a way to do it so, by all means, go out there and research the possibilities.

CASE STUDY

Her story

Whilst at work one day, I decided to open up a facebook page offering beauty advice. I built up quite a fan base over the next few years. I was often giving people recipes to make and they'd always ask if I could make it for them. It was then that I decided to set up an Etsy page. In 2014 I discovered I was pregnant with my second child. I left my job at my family's company for maternity leave but carried on making my beauty orders for as long as I could.

After I had the baby, I decided not to return to work. I was still getting plenty of business in for myself and I was given the perfect opportunity. Work from home in my own time whilst being able to focus on my baby. Since 2014 I have been a stay at home mum, but also working full time for myself. I'm so blessed to be in this situation. I am now pregnant with my third baby and lucky enough to be working from home and bringing in an income. Best of all I'm following my passion.

Zoe Bee, www.etsy.com/uk/shop/ZoeBeeBeauty

THE PRACTICALITIES OF SELF-EMPLOYMENT

Childcare

I mentioned childcare in Chapter 2, and that's where people expect it to be most relevant, but it's relevant whatever you decide to do. For instance, many women think about starting a home-based business with the belief that they'll do it alongside being a full-time mum. In other words, just do all their normal looking after baby stuff, fit in a few blog posts during nap times, update their social media on their phone in spare minutes and leave the important stuff until the evenings when the little one is tucked up in bed.

Please be realistic about what is achievable. Nap times can be erratic and sometimes won't fit in at all with the work you want to do. As your baby grows they'll take fewer and fewer naps until at some point between the ages of two and three, they will stop napping during the day altogether, so if you have managed to squeeze in a routine of working at those times, you're going to need to rearrange things pretty drastically when that happens. Domestic chores still need to be done, and aren't always achievable while your child is awake. Even if your partner is working but sharing the chores pretty evenly, you're still going to be tidying and cleaning up after yourself and the baby throughout the day, in addition to whatever your share of the housework is. Plus, if your baby isn't yet sleeping through the night then you're going to need some daytime nap time yourself. Not only that, but if you have been home all day, then please use your evenings to relax a bit, meet up with friends or spend time with your partner.

I'm not saying that if you're a full-time mum then you shouldn't try to build a business too. But building a business is hard work, as is being a full-time mum. What I'm saying is that if you're a full-time mum then you may find you have time to do a bit of work on the side, but don't kill yourself trying to build a multimillion pound company or working 50 hours a week. You are, of course, capable of doing that, but unless you can run your business entirely in the evenings (and depending on the type of work you do and how reliable your kids are at going to sleep, that's perfectly possible), you'll need childcare.

I know what it's like to sit with your kids willing them to go to sleep and then jump up, grab your laptop and start doing the client work you've been feeling guilty about not doing all day. It doesn't feel nice and if you're doing it regularly it's going to lead to burnout, not to mention some degree of resentment directed at either your kids or your partner.

I would say that all of the women I interviewed about their daily routine had introduced some form of childcare by the time their baby was a year old, even if it was just a few hours with a grandparent each week or an agreement that their partner deals with everything after 6pm. Even if you choose not to go back to work after maternity leave, there comes a point where maternity leave ends. If you choose to pursue a self-employed work-at-home career, you need to work out how you're going to balance your parenting role with your working role.

If you choose to be a full-time work-at-home mum, don't try to be a full-time mum too – accept a part-time role on one or the other. Get childcare sorted out for the times you're going to work. Your business will work best if you know in advance when you can work and how many hours a week. Otherwise you're just snatching snippets of time here and there and may never get enough time to immerse yourself in work mode. It does obviously depend on what kind of work you're doing, but say you're freelancing as a web designer, you're going to have to give clients estimates of when work will be done. Many clients will forgive a slipped deadline because of a one-off childcare emergency, but ongoing difficulties are not cool and they do nothing to demonstrate professionalism.

I want to stress here that you know your personal situation better than me. If your work can be done at any time of the day, and doesn't require face to face contact with a client, and if you can rely on your partner to deal with the children if they wake during your work time, then you could run a business entirely in the evening whilst being a full-time mum during the day.

It's okay to be a mum who works, but it's not okay to be a mum who consistently works while their child is with them and in need of attention. Yes, you can squeeze a bit of extra work in if your baby has a particularly long nap when you weren't expecting it, but you can't base your weekly workload on the unreliability of a tiny human's penchant for sleep. Don't put yourself in the position where you end up resenting having to 'deal with' your child instead of enjoying playing with them.

Many self-employed mums put off childcare because they think they can't afford it. And I do understand. The transition is hard. When you return to work, you know exactly how much money you're going to be paid each month and can plan your childcare bills accordingly. When you plan to leave your job and go freelance at the end of maternity leave you may have to organise childcare with no idea of how much you're going to earn or when you're going to get it. And even if you are going to a job with a known salary, you still want to reduce your childcare costs and maximise the amount of time you spend with your kids too. For childcare solutions please see Chapter 7.

Tax

Don't be put off by tax requirements if you're thinking of self-employment. It's quite straightforward and you don't have to register with HMRC right away, so you have time to actually get that business up and running before you need to start filing tax returns.

Finances are not my speciality and I'm definitely not qualified to give any kind of financial advice, but I seem to manage so I'm sure you will too. The rules are always changing, so please take everything I'm about to say as general guidance which needs to be checked before you act on it. You need to register as self-employed by the month of October following the tax year in which you started your business. In other words, if you started freelancing in June 2016, you would need to register with HMRC by October 2017 and file a tax return for the April 2016 – April 2017 tax year before 31 January 2018. As part of your tax returns you will also need to pay National Insurance contributions if your profit is over £6000 per year. If your profit is lower you don't have to pay anything, but you could choose to pay voluntary contributions if you're worried about gaps in your NI record (which can affect your state pension entitlement).

I would advise you to get some accounting software (there are free ones available) or at the very least a spreadsheet to keep track of incomings and outgoings related to your self-employment activities. I think it is also helpful to speak to an accountant at some point even if you choose not to employ them on an ongoing basis. They can advise you on what expenses you can charge to your business, anything you need to know about registering with HMRC, and other practical money questions you may have. It's not a requirement of self-employment that you hire or even speak to an accountant, but I know I felt more confident about what would be expected of me in terms of taxes and self-assessment once I'd spoken to an expert.

When it is time to file your tax return, don't leave it until the end of January and risk missing the deadline. If you really struggle with doing it yourself, there are plenty of accountants or bookkeepers out there who will do it for a one-off fee but, again, don't wait until January to contact them.

CHAPTER 6

Doing Something Else

Up until now I've looked at going back to work in various forms, becoming a full-time mum and starting different kinds of businesses. But what if none of these appeal to you? Or you want to supplement being a full-time mum or part-time worker with something else? The ongoing theme throughout this book, as you've probably realised by now, is to use maternity leave as a time of renewal and reinvention to change the course of your life. Just because you're successful in a career doesn't mean it's the right choice to go back to the same career. Maybe now is the time to try something completely different.

I will now present a few ideas which worked surprisingly well for me.

BLOGGING

I wouldn't be surprised if 'blogger' had overtaken 'novelist' as the top dream career. When I was at school everyone wanted to be a novelist, but then of course blogging didn't exist. Now it very much does and everyone wants to have a blog – far easier than crafting a whole novel. Bloggers just sit down and write about their lives and earn loads of money for doing it, don't they?

Well, the somewhat predictable truth of the matter is that it isn't that easy or that simple.

What makes a blog successful?

The first thing to understand – and this may be obvious to you and it seems common sense, but so many people don't seem to get it – the writing doesn't make the money. It's the additional stuff you do with your blog that makes money. And that doesn't mean advertising either, certainly not the Google AdWords variety anyway. Lots of people when they set up their brand new blog get excited that they can add adverts to it and earn money for no work other than putting in a tiny bit of code. Please don't do this. The amount you'll earn will be pennies yet the bad user experience for your readers is likely to stop many of them returning.

Which leads to my next point about blogging. The only way to make money from blogging is to have lots of readers. Lots of readers means that you can attract some carefully chosen advertisers, with well-designed ads that complement rather than clash with your blog's ethos and brand, and who pay a flat rate directly to you for having an ad on your site. Or you may find companies to 'sponsor' a post (i.e. pay you money to write a post that puts their product in a good light). Sponsoring of posts is very popular in the 'mum blog' space with baby products suppliers falling over themselves to get reviews of their products in front of thousands of parents. Lots of readers also means that when you write an e-course or a book based on your blog, you have an audience who will already be interested in buying it and a platform to build on.

Finally, lots of readers means you can benefit from affiliate marketing, which is where you get a commission for referring people to a particular programme or product. All you have to do is write a relevant post and embed your unique link into it or create an ad box or banner which links to the product.

For a blog to make money, a combination of some or even all of these methods are used. In fact, if you also add in the odd service, like ghost-writing content for other people's blogs, then your 'blogging' becomes a business of the type we discussed in the previous chapter. So really, in order to make money from a blog, you need to treat it as a tool of your business. Which means at some point you need to work out a target market and create posts that appeal to that market.

But yes, I know, I know, you just want to express your creativity and write about whatever you like, when you like. And that's fine if the blog is just for you. But if you have aspirations to turn your blog into a money-making venture then you need to start thinking in terms of who is reading it and start writing it for them. A blog full of random posts about your family life is unlikely to appeal to many outside of your own immediate family. But start to hone in a little and blog about a certain element of your life and you will find people in the same boat flock to you.

There are plenty of 'mum blogs' out there which cover the trials and tribulations of being a mum. Many are humorous – as many successful blogs are – or heart-wrenching. If you're going to do a mum blog, think about your angle. It could be something to do with working and parenting, raising twins, raising a child with a specific medical condition, or anything else. The possibilities are endless. Just make sure you choose something that you actually enjoy writing about and that you feel comfortable sharing. If you want to blog about your child's medical condition, for instance, but feel stressed and upset every time you write about it, then perhaps it's not the right subject for your blog or maybe now just isn't the right time to be doing it.

Getting started

All blogs start with virtually no readers. The only way to get readers is to make your blog so good that people will take time out of their day to read a post or two, enjoy it and share it for other people to read. It's no good sharing it and asking others to share it as a favour – that'll soon fizzle out. It's only when you find strangers tweeting it or sharing it with their friends that it will start to snowball into a blog with a high readership.

But to maintain a high readership, they have to have something to read. Which means you need to write often and consistently. Nothing kills a new reader's interest in a blog more than happening upon a good post only to find out from a quick search that there haven't been any new posts for a couple of months. They're likely to leave and never return – they'll assume you're not doing it anymore. Which means that for a while, and for some this can be many months, you will have to write posts and share them and repeat and on and on even though your stats may be showing you that virtually no one is reading.

That can be hard on your self-confidence and a couple of months after starting is when most people give up. It starts with skipping a week because no one will notice anyway. Then maybe another week. Then an apology post about how you haven't written in a while. Apology posts are not cool – they alert future readers to the fact that you might be a bit scatty when it comes to posting and that you may well disappear again. And then, when no one has commented about your absence you start to be absent more often, until it's been six months since you last wrote a post and you can't think of anything new to write about anyway.

It's sad, I know. So please, if you decide to get into blogging, don't take that downward spiral to obscurity. Keep it up and have faith in yourself to keep going through the readerless phase. Write well, make it interesting for others, share posts in spaces where your ideal readers hang out and you could become Internet famous.

Guest posting

Sharing in spaces where your ideal readers hang out is one key strategy for making you more visible. The other big one is to guest post on relevant blogs. Don't view similar blogs as yours as competition, see them as potential platforms. Some of the bigger blogs have open requests for guest contributors and they publish submission guidelines. If that's the case then follow the guidelines and submit a post. If the blog is smaller or doesn't have any obvious contribution guidelines, contact the blogger and ask if you can write something for them.

A rule of thumb here is to be mindful that you're not wasting anyone's time. Before you contact someone directly, check that they haven't got a statement about not accepting contributions on their site somewhere. If they have submission guidelines, follow them to the letter. Read lots of posts, not just the latest one, so you can get a feel for the tone of writing, the number of guest posts, the length of typical posts and the relevance of what you want to write. When you pitch your idea, don't be so vague that they have to ask you for more details before saying yes or no. Tell them the title of the post, what it's about and how long it is. Give them enough information so they can decide whether they want to work with you or not.

The Huffington Post is a great place to start because it's a well-respected site that most people have heard of and yet it's not that difficult to get accepted to write blogs for them. At the beginning of 2014, I stuck the Huffington Post logo on my list of goals I wanted to achieve that year and was fully prepared to make several attempts to get published. Three weeks into January my first submission was accepted and I was already up there. Since then, lots of people have asked me about getting published on the HuffPo and the reality is that all you have to do is write a good post and then approach them with it. You can find a link to a more detailed post I wrote about how to get published on HuffPo in the Resources section.

The final thing to say about guest blogging to build your own readership is that once you have a post up on someone else's blog, make sure it's accompanied by a good author bio and a link back to your own blog.

Blogging tends to be a slow burner and most well-known blogs were small for ages before blowing up and becoming well-known. If you do start writing a blog during maternity leave, it could be something you continue after you return to work or while you work as a full-time mum, with the aim of regularly writing and chipping away at gradually increasing readers until such time as it starts to produce an income for you.

PODCASTING

I've separated this out from blogging and service-based businesses, but really it's very similar. A podcast itself is a free product – like a blog post but in audio form. People don't pay to listen to the podcast, but if you have enough listeners, you can approach one or two companies to sponsor your show. This means they pay you an amount of money (and this is something you ask for depending on how much value you think you can give them – the more listeners you have, the more you can charge) to have a jingle, advert or shout-out about their company in your show.

A podcast should also have a website to go alongside it, so all the things I mentioned in the blogging section about earning money from your blog apply equally to the website that holds your podcast.

Podcasts can have many different formats – single host, co-hosts, interviews, news or documentary style reports – so your first task would be to decide what topic you want to cover and in what format you want to do it.

One of the easiest ways to grow a podcast is to interview people on your show or be interviewed on other shows – this is the equivalent of guest posting for bloggers. When you interview someone you immediately have another person who is invested in getting as many people as they can to listen to that episode, so they'll be sharing the link with their friends and audience. It's a bit of a win-win if you both have big audiences because each of you can benefit from the exposure to each other's followers. But interview podcasts have the downside of finding people to interview and the practicalities of arranging times when both of you are available – a tough one if you're home with a baby and you don't know in advance when you're going to be free to talk. Some kind of online scheduling app is useful to avoid to-ing and fro-ing emails about timings and, if you do plan to do a regular interview show, it's a good idea to batch up all your interviews to happen on specific days of the week so you can spend the rest of your time editing and scheduling episodes for publication.

Equipment for podcasting doesn't have to be expensive and difficult to learn, so don't be put off by technology, but do make it a priority to make your recording quality the best it can be. A good microphone and a quiet room are essential. If you're doing interviews then a fast and reliable Internet connection and recording software to work with Skype are also crucial. It's also worth learning the basics about tagging your files with correct metadata before uploading to iTunes or other podcasting platforms.

For around six months in 2014 I hosted a weekly podcast for the Maternity Leavers blog. Each week I interviewed a woman who had changed her career after having children, so this book is partly inspired by that podcast. As an interviewer I loved meeting so many inspirational women and learning about how they managed everything day-to-day, and why they'd made the life choices they had. But the sheer amount of time that it took to schedule, record, edit, fluff and publish the episodes – not to mention writing summaries of each episode as a shareable blog post on the website – was unsustainable for me. It was exhausting work and despite having a few very loyal listeners, it wasn't a roaring success in terms of listener numbers. And without what I considered to be adequate listener numbers, I didn't feel confident approaching potential sponsors.

But despite my low success in podcasting I would recommend it highly as a form of communication and for the experience you get from it. For instance, I used to spend hours editing 'ums' out of my podcast until I stopped because it just took too long. Instead, I learnt some techniques to stop myself humming, and I'm now a much better speaker and presenter.

Don't be put off because you don't like the sound of your own voice. So many people get really uncomfortable listening to themselves, but it really is all in your mind. When I managed to cut down my 'ums', I don't think anyone noticed much. They were mostly listening to what I was saying and not paying attention to my trip ups.

I love podcasting. Partly because I love talking and it gave me the perfect opportunity to do just that, but also because it's one thing getting your voice out there in the form of a blog post, but literally getting my voice out there felt, for me at least, so much more personal and brave. I hope I'll do another show one day.

WRITING A BOOK

Blogging is probably more popular than writing a book simply because it's easier and the results, if you get any, are more immediate. But lots of people still want to be a writer or a novelist, and maternity leave feels like the perfect time to sit down and write that book you've been subconsciously planning on the train to work every day.

The great news is that there's no one and nothing stopping you. Writing a book is a perfect thing to do since all it requires is pockets of quiet time and access to a computer. I know of people who have used the crèche at their local gym to do an hours' writing here and there while their child gets a bit of playtime. Or people who write 1,000 (or 500 or 2,000) words every evening or each morning before the rest of the house wakes up. I know of people who write only at naptimes and otherwise don't really think about it for the rest of their day.

The pocket of time you find might be as little as 10 minutes or as much as several hours. Either one is fine. When writing this book, I sometimes wrote no more than 50 words in several hours while I procrastinated and faffed around finding all sorts of other things to occupy my time, and on other occasions (usually about 20 minutes before I had to be at school to pick up my kids) I could knock out 500 words in no time at all. We all work in different ways.

Apart from finding the time to write – which you will, if you want to – the big questions are:

1. What are you going to write about? Will it be a novel or a non-fiction book? What genre or topic will you focus on?
2. Are you going to self-publish or pitch to publishers?

On the second point, there is plenty of advice out there on which option would be best for you, so I won't go into it here, other than to say don't rule out either option too early on and don't put off starting because you're still deciding. Either way you're going to have to write the book, so start now and decide down the line what feels like a good fit for you.

If you're writing a fiction book you'll need to finish writing it before you can send your submission off to agents or publishers anyway, so don't think of anything other than the story until you're some way through actually writing it.

For non-fiction books, do your homework first and check your idea hasn't already been done. It isn't unknown for people to pitch publishers with ideas that closely resemble current bestsellers. Make sure that isn't you! You need a new idea, or a new angle on an idea, and you need to be clear about who your market is. What type of person will buy the book? Who are you writing it for? Regardless of whether you self-publish or pitch to a publisher, there's no point in writing a book if there's no market for it.

If you're writing a non-fiction book and you want to go down the traditional publishing route, it is possible to pitch it to publishers before the book is finished. However, it will likely help your case to be some way along the writing journey before you submit your proposal. Approaching a publisher with nothing written at all doesn't put you in a very strong pitching position, though be aware that if a publisher accepts your idea, they may suggest a different angle. The publisher will expect to see a book proposal, comprising a brief outline of the book, the audience you are aiming it at, a short author biography and the book's introduction, as well as either a few sample chapters or a chapter-by-chapter outline, so you'll need to have all that figured out before you propose anything. The best way to do that is to have written at least an outline or first draft. A final note to bear in mind is that not all publishing houses accept unsolicited submissions so do research the submissions process before you send anything anywhere. But the particular process of a particular publisher should not stop you from starting.

What I'm saying is to get on with it and worry about the ins and outs of publishing once you're further along. Yes, you will want to research whether to submit a book proposal or self-publish, but don't use that research as an excuse not to start writing.

Top Three Writing Tips

1. **Try to write something every day**, even if it's just 100 words in the five minutes before you head to bed. It keeps the project going mentally even if it's moving forward very slowly. Although writing a book can take people months or even years, it doesn't have to be a mammoth task if you don't let it be. Many non-fiction books are around 50,000 to 75,000 words long. If you managed to write 1,000 words each day, you'd hit the lower end of that range in just a couple of months.

2. **Give yourself regular targets**: I find a word count target for each day is helpful. I take into account the amount of time I have available, the topic I'm writing that day and whether it's something I'm struggling with or should be able to steam through. My target usually ranges from 1,000 to 4,000 words a day. You might prefer a time target – aim to spend, say, one hour at your desk or writing solidly for 30 minutes at the coffee shop. Whatever you choose, make it fit your situation and make it realistic, but if you don't reach your target just move on to the next day without beating yourself up.
3. **An ultimate deadline is helpful too** – the date by which you will have finished a first draft, a second draft or your editing. If you're feeling really confident, you could book in your copy-editor, proof-reader or even printer ahead of time so that you absolutely have to finish everything by a certain date. If you're going through a publisher rather than self-publishing, other people will set these deadlines for you and that usually makes it easier (if a tad more stressful) to stick to.

One of the great things about writing a book is that it's a stand-alone project. It's not as all-encompassing as starting a business and not as open-ended as starting a blog. It's something very clear to aim towards and I think makes a great maternity leave project.

The downside is that it's not a long-term plan in itself,

because the opportunities that arise out of it are unpredictable. You might be fortunate enough to write a novel which becomes a bestseller, subsequently attract a new book deal and choose to leave your job in order to write more books, but this is by no means the most common experience. If you make a lot of money directly from writing a book then you're one of the fortunate few, but a good non-fiction book might have other benefits – it could turn out to be the perfect way to attract clients into your new business or get you a fantastic new job or promotion.

If you feel that writing a book is for you, though, get on and do it and see where it leads.

CASE STUDY

Her story

I'd planned to write a novel set in Renaissance Italy during my maternity leave, but I was in the baby zone and started to edit all the wonderful baby advice my mum – health visitor Sarah Beeson MBE – was giving to me and my friends on a daily basis. We soon realised we had a first-year parenting advice book that was not only practical but had a gentle focus on your baby's emotional development and how challenging but wondrous life can be as a new parent. By the time I was due to return to work we had a first draft of Happy Baby, Happy Family.

I put together a proposal with the best four chapters, a synopsis and market research to test the water to see if we could find a home for our book. Straight away we had interest from small independent publishers because you can contact them directly, while you need an agent to represent you with some of the bigger publishers who often don't take unsolicited manuscripts. I sent our pitch to a literary agent I'd been introduced to in a pub by author Paul Magrs before I was even a mum. I remember sending that email at 11 o'clock on a Sunday night days before I was due to return to work and dreading that I'd never hear back. But bright and early the next morning he'd emailed me back with the news he wanted to sign us.

Once we'd signed with our agent he showed the manuscript and proposal to the top publishing houses. We had several offers and accepted a three-book deal with HarperCollins who not only wanted Happy Baby, Happy Family but two memoirs of Mum's early life training to be a nurse in Hackney and being a young newly-qualified health visitor in a country village in the 1970s.

I went back to my job for six months and by the time I left the book deal was done. With three books to write and a baby to look after I handed in my notice and set up my own micro communications business Wordsby and got to work. Three years on it's been an amazing journey. Writing and meeting readers is definitely the highlight for me. I've most enjoyed working on the novels The New Arrival and Our Country Nurse, but getting to coo over other people's babies when we meet parents at events is rather lovely. I never imagined my first books would be with my mum but it's been a huge blessing – I've learnt so much.

Amy Beeson, co-author of *Our Country Nurse*, *The New Arrival* and *Happy Baby, Happy Family*, owner of wordsbycommunications.com

EDUCATION AND RETRAINING

Have you ever felt that urge to learn something new or go back to study 'some day'? Perhaps you wanted to go to college when you were younger but it didn't fit into your life or maybe you went to university but have since thought about doing some postgraduate study. Perhaps formal education just didn't agree with you when you were younger but now you're intrigued to give it another go.

It doesn't have to be something as high commitment as university. It could be a part-time GCSE or A level or a vocational course. Perhaps you think learning a trade would be a good plan – why not train to be a plumber or electrician? There are lots of careers we write off earlier in life because we haven't got the right qualifications. What if your maternity leave was the perfect opportunity to enrol on a course and start on the path to your dream career?

For instance, say you're almost certain that you're going to stay at home to look after your baby. You've discussed it with your husband and you both agree that you'll stay at home full-time until your child starts school. During those few years you could make good headway on an Open University degree. Or even start and finish a distance learning master's.

The Internet offers you so many options for self-study that you may never need to set foot in an actual educational institution, unless you want to. The number of courses on offer is almost endless and, while costs vary wildly between a GCSE at your local college and a PhD at a prestigious university, there's likely to be something that suits your budget, location and level of current education.

If university is your choice, there are loans available to cover tuition fees and/or living expenses for both undergraduate and postgraduate courses. If you've never been to university and don't even have A levels that doesn't have to be a barrier, as mature student requirements are mostly non-academic. Most banks offer some sort of career development loan for non-university courses and, if you're thinking of retraining for a specific career, check out what bursaries and sponsorships may be available to support you.

My experience

I started university way back in 2000 at the ripe old age of 21. I didn't have A levels thanks to a bit of a teenage rebellion which saw me asked to leave school at the end of year 12. So I went to the local further education college to do a course in media studies. I loved the practical elements of this course. I spent hours locked away in the darkroom developing photos from scratch (a skill of much use in today's digital world!) and yet more hours in the radio studio writing and reading the news reports and presenting popular shows.

As an aside here, writing, photography and presenting were interests and skills that have never left me and, later in life, when I looked back at what I could do if I could do anything, I identified these as things I wanted to weave into whatever career would come next for me. Thinking back over what really made me tick gave me a good indicator of where my passions lie. Sometimes our passions are buried so deep we can't find them so it's great to find a time like this in your life when you really excelled at something.

Ultimately, though, two distinction level optional modules and an awful lot of unfinished (not to mention unstarted) mandatory projects does not make for an overall pass. I put even less work into this course than I had with my A levels, so it was unsurprising that by the end of it I achieved a spectacular fail and for the second time in my life I was asked to leave an educational establishment in disgrace and with no new qualifications.

But after a couple of years of work under my belt, the call to study was strong. I was disillusioned in my office job – a situation that unfortunately I would come to know again and again over the next 15 years or so. But during hours of research at the local library in my lunch breaks (I know, you'd use the Internet now, but this was 1999 and the Internet was still a novelty), I found out that universities usually accepted 'mature students' with little or no qualifications if they could demonstrate their ability in some other way. I knew all about mature students, of course, I mean, who hasn't seen *Educating Rita*? But I thought you had to be older than I was – by now the ripe old age of 20. But in fact all you had to be was 21. So the following year I started my degree as a full-time mature student, and am happy to report that I finally finished a programme of study without being kicked out. This was an important lesson to me about not just accepting what you always believed. I had assumed university was off limits to me without actually giving it much thought.

After many more years of work, and becoming a parent and then getting divorced, I went through another stage of 'What do I want to do with my life?' This lesson reared its head again in the form of ruling out postgraduate study because I always thought it would be too expensive. Then, early in 2016 as I was doing some self-discovery and realised I wanted my next project to be a master's, a new postgraduate student loan was introduced. So despite not having done academic study for several years and having assumed I would never be able to afford it, I'm now studying an MSc in Criminology.

Never rule anything out, and look for the loophole, exception or extenuating circumstances in any course of action where you don't fit the usual criteria. If you're asked for specific qualifications in order to qualify for a job or study course, always see if relevant work experience or an alternative qualification will do instead.

But university may not be right for you – you may in the end decide that the fees are too high or the commitment greater than you're willing to devote right now. Check out other options like adult education programmes at local colleges or short summer courses held at a nearby university. Vocational courses are a good idea, with many leading to specific careers or including opportunities for work experience.

One career option which has been popular among mums

I've spoken to is to train as an instructor in something. Pilates, yoga or personal training are great if you're already part of that world and go to classes yourself. Kids swimming instructor is another popular one. These are all careers which might allow you to pick up a few hours' work a week on a self-employed basis at your local leisure centre or take up as a full- or part-time employed job. It doesn't have to be fitness-related though; think computer skills training or professional development programmes as well.

FEARS WHICH MIGHT ARISE

A common fear that crops up around retraining or re-joining education as a mature student is that you feel too far out of touch and that you need to catch up before you embark on a course of study. This may be true to an extent, but you'd be surprised how much comes back to you once you get going. It wouldn't hurt to do a bit of extra reading if it's a brand-new subject to you, but don't put something off because you're worried about not being as good as everyone else. You almost certainly will be as good, if not better than your fellow students, especially if you're bringing life experiences (like being a parent, for instance) that they haven't yet had.

Not having enough time is another fear, but often more of an excuse than a fear. It's true you may have less leisure time now you're a parent, and you have to balance caring for your kids with domestic chores and possibly professional work too.

I'm sure there are people who really don't have time to add study to their mix, but ruling anything out with an outright 'I don't have time' is usually a mistake. When you really want something, you'll find the time. You may have to give up other things, but most people can find a few hours of TV to ditch or spend a little less time faffing on the Internet.

I say this, but I also don't want you to pressure yourself into taking on more than you can handle. The best thing to do is sit down and draw up a timetable. Be realistic about how many hours a week commitment is needed on a particular course, taking into account both classes and home study, and then add in your personal commitments. You may well find there is time. Or you may satisfy yourself that there isn't, but maybe there will be when the kids are a bit older, in which case park it as a future plan.

Finally, don't forget that a course might be only for a few months or a year, so you only have to sustain the time juggling for a finite time. It's amazing how quickly that time goes, but how life-changing the investment is when you're qualified to begin a totally new career.

TRADING AND MATCHED BETTING

Trading might seem like an unusual thing to include here, but I know quite a few mums who do it or have tried it. When I say trading, you may immediately think of investment banks and the stock exchange and decide that's far too risky and difficult for someone with absolutely no experience whatsoever. But hear me out. Financial trading is a thing, yes, and you can trade on the stock exchange. But you can also trade on the FOREX (foreign currencies) market or you can do sports trading (using the betting exchange to trade on whether odds shorten or lengthen on sport matches).

One of the things I love about trading is that it appeals to my inner introvert and allows me a way to make money which doesn't involve leaving the house or seeing anyone. What drew me to trading after years of blogging, writing and trying to build an email list, was that you don't need any of that. There's no marketing, there's no selling to customers, there's no emotive copywriting involved. It's just you and the screen, and a bit of brainwork. On top of that, some forms of trading are perfect to do around kids' schedules as you can dip in and out during nap times and evenings, and even automate things to work while you're not in front of the computer (although be careful and only automate when you know what you're doing!). And, honestly, it's not that hard to learn the basics. After that it's experience and practice which makes you good at it.

I do speak from a bit of experience here, as with most of the ideas in this book. It so happens that I dabbled in a bit of sports trading which I got into via something called matched betting which is similar but risk-free. I'll tell you a bit about both because they're distinct but similar; in one I was very successful while in the other, not so much.

Matched betting

Let's start with matched betting, as that's what I started on. Matched betting works on the premise that online bookmakers – like Ladbrokes or William Hill – will give away 'free bets' to new and existing customers. They do this, of course, to encourage you to bet more. So when you join a bookmaker's site they'll offer, say, a £50 free bet if you place a £10 bet with your own money first. If you were planning to have a little flutter on the horses, that's a great offer, because even if you lose your initial bet, you have another chance of winning big with that £50 bet and you never have to risk more than a tenner. That would likely entice you to use that bookie above another perhaps. So, they all offer variations on 'place a bet and we'll give you a free bet as a thank you for choosing us'.

In matched betting, you join several sites and you use the offers on all of them. But how can you make sure you don't have an unlucky streak and lose all your initial qualifying bets? That's where the betting exchange comes in. There are a few different exchanges, but the main one is Betfair. At a bookie you would usually bet on an outcome, so you'd bet on Shergar to win a horse race or you'd bet on Plymouth Argyle to win a football match. If they lose, you lose your bet. But on Betfair, you can also bet against outcomes, so you could bet on Shergar not winning his race or on Plymouth Argyle not winning their match. (A bet against is called a 'lay bet' or 'laying'.)

So you join Ladbrokes and bet £10 on Plymouth Argyle

to win tonight's match, then you go on to Betfair and place a lay bet of £10 on Plymouth Argyle to not win. Whatever the outcome, you win your bet either at Ladbrokes or at Betfair, because they're either going to win or not win (i.e. lose or draw). When the match is over, you have broken even. If you won the bet at the bookie, you lost around the same amount at Betfair and vice versa. But what you have earned from this no-risk process is a free £50 bet. Now when you place that £50 bet at the bookie on another sporting event and lay it at Betfair, the money you win – usually around £40 on a £50 free bet – is pure profit. Repeat that at different bookies on different days with different offers and you can make quite a bit of money.

A couple of things to note, however. I'm keeping it very simple here and sticking to the concepts rather than the detailed how-tos. If you've never heard of matched betting before now and you don't know how the betting exchange works, then you don't have everything you need to get started from my brief explanation of what it is. My outline is so you can see whether it's a concept you think you might like to give a go.

When I started matched betting I joined a membership site which has videos training you in the process and a calculator to help you work out how much to bet depending on the odds available. I paid (and still do pay) around £20 a month to be a member of this site where they update daily the latest offers alongside detailed instructions. In my opinion it's worth the investment as I can make that money back on the first day of each month. Some months that's all I do, while in other months I make a few hundred quid on top. I've included a link in the Resources section so you can learn more about the site I use but there are plenty of others and you're welcome to do a Google search for them. Even though I no longer need instructions for the straightforward offers it's worth the fee to have someone out there testing which offers are live at which bookmaker, to have a calculator configured to work out exactly how much money to place on each bet under what circumstances and the forum where people discuss any issues they've had in doing the offers.

Secondly, although if done right there is no risk, you do need to have a bit of money in the betting exchange in order to lay the bet. The reason is because when you lay a bet (i.e. bet against an outcome) what you're doing in effect is betting for any of the other outcomes to happen. So, in a horse race, to bet on a horse to win may cost you £10, but to bet against him to win it may cost you £50 as you're covering all eventualities. The actual figures vary depending on the odds (price) of the horse. So in the same way that you win more if you bet on an outsider rather than the favourite, it will cost you more to lay a horse that is not likely to win. Again, trying not to get into specifics, a rule of thumb is that if you want to get into matched betting you'll want a few hundred quid to use for placing lay bets at the exchange. You'll get it back, sometimes within minutes, but you do need to put it up there in the first place.

That said, I started with less than £100, managed to place a few bets and win another £100 and I was able to build it up pretty quickly. If you aim to use your first month of winnings as your bank and keep it in the system, then you'll be on to a great start. As a guide, I made £700 in my first month (spending a couple of hours a day on it) and then settled at about half of that in subsequent months once I'd run through the welcome offers and started spending less time on it. Still, a few hundred quid a month for a few hours work a week is not a bad return I reckon.

Sports trading

From matched betting I moved on to sports trading, which is a different kettle of fish because here your money is at risk. Now, this isn't a bad thing in itself – almost everything we do requires some level of risk: changing jobs, starting a business, having a baby. But with sports trading you're taking these risks several times a day every day that you're doing it. For some people that isn't a state of mind that they'll enjoy. And for others who like a good gamble, it may not be good for them either. Trading is gambling. The thing with trading that is different to betting is that you tend to make lots of small gains over a high number of trades instead of hoping to win big from a small number of bets. With sports trading you don't really bet on the outcome – you're trading based on how you think the market will fluctuate in reaction to certain events.

In contrast to the matched betting where you're using bookies and relying on the offers available, when you trade on Betfair you're trading solely on that one platform. The aim is to place a bet on an outcome, say Plymouth Argyle winning a football match, and then lay that bet when the price is lower. That way, whatever the outcome, you make a profit on the difference between those two prices. In fact most trades are done and dusted before the event even starts – the outcome is unimportant. Your money is won or lost based on how the odds on each eventuality go up and down in the run up to the match.

Again, I'm simplifying because this isn't a book on how to trade. I just want you to get a feel for what it is so that you can decide if it's something you'd like to learn more about. With trading, you will need more money than with matched betting – about £1000 would be a good start. And you will need to practise either in training mode or with tiny stakes as you grow in confidence. I wouldn't recommend jumping in like you can with matched betting after watching a few videos. In fact, most traders I know (including myself) start with a few months of matched betting before moving on to trading when they fully understand how the betting exchange works.

My experience with trading was short-lived, I'll be honest, but I did enjoy it. The adrenaline rush on winning a trade – even one for just a couple of quid – was brilliant. Overall, I still turned a profit over the course of a few months. But, despite that, I don't feel I have the right mentality for trading or perhaps I could do but I need to hone it better. The secret to successful trading is simple: discipline. Unfortunately, this isn't one of my strongest traits! I relied far too heavily on hoping as a strategy, but it sadly doesn't play much of a useful role in trading. That said, I learnt a great deal from trading about my attitude to money, to risk and to discipline. It's an experience I'm very glad I tried and a skill I'm very glad I have – I can still spot opportunities to make a quick buck from a certain kind of tennis match, for instance.

However, when it boiled down to it, I took too many risks on trades that I could see weren't worth doing, let too many small losses build into bigger losses because of my penchant for eternal optimism and I chased after big wins instead of building my bank up safely and steadily with small surer wins. Ultimately, I'm too much of a hothead to do trading for any prolonged length of time, but that doesn't mean it's not right for other people. Perhaps you'll fare better.

As for other types of trading, like FOREX, I don't have experience of them, although I suspect the lessons I've learnt will be relevant there too. Trading is about discipline. If you're not willing or able to develop that discipline, then you probably won't make a good trader.

Other things to try similar to trading might be poker playing or the low-risk offers in online casinos. Many of the bookies have slots or casinos on their site, and taking up offers is less risky than playing normally. I did these kinds of offers alongside the matched betting and they're included in the membership site I mentioned. It's not no-risk, but it can be low-risk – you can choose to do only those offers with a maximum risk of, say, £10. So you either lose that £10 or you win an unspecified amount. As long as you don't risk more than you're comfortable losing (an important rule of thumb for any betting, gambling or trading scenario) then risking the odd tenner here and there might be worth it.

I once spent £2 of my own money on a bingo game to match a free £2 bonus. In a room of nearly 1,000 people I won the house and walked away with £260. Not bad for a couple of quid and a game which I left to auto run while I went and bathed my kids. The winning can be fun, the losing not so much, but I have to admit to quite liking it when people ask me what I do, to tell them I'm a mum, writer, student and professional gambler. It certainly gets the conversation going!

CHAPTER 7

Money and Practicalities

It's all very well daydreaming about all the things we could do with our lives, and I totally recommend that for a while, but at some point we need to deal with the practical elements of making our dreams into reality.

Everyone has so many unique practical responsibilities and no book could cover everything for everyone, but I'm going to look at a few key things that you'll need to sort out during or after your maternity leave.

This section is pretty much all focused on the UK system so if you're not in the UK, feel free to skip the bits which don't apply to you.

BENEFITS

Check out which benefits and schemes you may be entitled to. You've probably heard this from other people, my midwives were always saying it to me, but if you've been in a well-paid job and never claimed any kind of benefits before, you may be surprised at what you're entitled to once you become a parent, particularly if your income drops while on maternity leave or disappears due to you not returning to work.

Child Benefit is the best known one, but there are also tax credits for those who work and for those who don't. Eligibility rules vary from benefit to benefit and from year to year – it's harder to keep track of than the advice for whether to move your baby on to solid food at four or six months! I'm therefore not going to go into details about specifics, as even the two I've mentioned will probably have changed by the time this book is published. Suffice to say, unless you're on a very high salary and your maternity pay is the same as that salary, then it may be worth some calculations on the government's website to see what you could be eligible for.

If you have to pay for any childcare, find out what your employer offers in the way of childcare vouchers. Again, this particular scheme is likely at some point to be consigned to the annals of history, so if that's happened by the time you read this, there'll hopefully be something else in its place. At the time of writing, the amount of childcare vouchers you could get can affect your tax credits entitlement, so the government has a handy calculator to work out which one you'd be better off claiming. Of course, everything changes for each year your baby ages, so that by the time they're a toddler or pre-schooler, you'll be able to get free nursery hours too.

In summary, read the government website and use the online

benefits calculators (see Resources section).

SHARED PARENTAL LEAVE

It is now possible in the UK for men to get substantial amounts of time off work to care for their child, which means that the onus is no longer on the mother to take a career break. Theoretically what this should mean is that discrimination is reduced because employers can't just assume anymore that a woman will have more time off around the birth of a child than her male colleagues, who are equally as likely to ask for extended time off. It should also mean that couples can plan for them both to play the role of full-time parent, even if only for a limited amount of time.

The reality is that use of the scheme is much lower than the government predicted and those who have taken it up have only had a couple of months off. Clearly this is not in the same ballpark as a woman taking 12 months off, so it's unlikely to have much impact on the discrimination issue for now.

The rules of shared parental leave are quite complex and are likely to change in the future, so look them up and familiarise yourself with all aspects of it before making any firm decisions or handing in notices to either yours or your partner's employers. At the time of writing the basic overview is that when the mother ends her maternity leave, any time left of the 52 weeks she's entitled to can be taken as parental leave in up to three blocks by either parent up until their child is one.

I believe that taking shared parental leave is a good thing

for individual families and for society. If the mum goes back to work and the dad can stay home, even if only for a month, he gets a feel for what it's like to be at home on your own with your child all day. This understanding is vital for building good strong relationships between parents. And if the woman is the higher earner before a couple become parents, then she is free to continue her work while the lower earning man takes a cut in income.

If more men are home with their kids – not just at weekends when they're not working, but being home instead of working full-time – then it's likely that more services and support will be geared towards male full-time parents. This is especially important for those of us who choose the route of going back to work and leaving our partner in charge of childcare. When I went back to work (before shared parental leave was introduced, unfortunately) my husband found it quite difficult to find baby groups and sessions that he felt welcome at. They were all full of mums who either took pity on him for being abandoned by his wife or were condescending towards him, praising him for managing to get the babies dressed and out of the house despite him being a man.

If we're going to expect that the work of childcare can be shared between parents of both gender, then we need to treat full-time dads no differently to full-time mums. Hopefully if more and more families choose to take advantage of shared parental leave, or give men a larger role in childcare, then men with babies won't be seen as such a novelty and we can all just get on with the hard job of parenting.

I'll get off my soapbox now! From a practical point of view, you need to discuss with your partner whether shared parental leave is something you want to include in your post maternity leave plans and, if so, find out whether you and your partner are eligible for it. As with the benefits section, head over to the government website where you'll find all the criteria along with a handy calculator to help you work out the costs or savings of doing it (see Resources section).

CHILDCARE SOLUTIONS

If you decide to return to work or become self-employed, then you will need to find someone to look after your child while you are working. The most ideal situation with childcare is to try and balance time with your children between you and your partner as much as possible. So if either of you has the option to work compressed hours, shorter hours or any other kind of flexible working arrangement that can tie in with the other one, then that's great. I know families where both parents work four-day weeks and take different days off so they only have to pay for nursery three days a week. You could also experiment with one of you starting late and the other finishing early, or any number of other combinations that reduce time spent at nursery and therefore the cost of childcare. Any free childcare you can get is ideal – so grandparents, siblings or friends who are already home with babies of their own are also an option (though it's a big ask, it may work out in some situations, especially if you can return the favour by babysitting for them on other days).

Aside from these free options, the most popular place for childcare is a nursery. They tend to come in two types:

1. The term time only preschool, which is usually attached to a school and may not take kids until they're two or three.
2. Day nurseries which run every weekday (sometimes even weekends) throughout the year regardless of school terms.

One of the problems of this kind of childcare is that it's often inflexible. Once your child is enrolled in, you have to pay every week regardless of sickness or absence, and usually in advance. This is fine if you want a long-term arrangement, but not so great if you only need a couple of weeks here and there as you switch from working on one project to a different one with different working hours required.

At a crèche you can pay for sessions without committing to whole terms of upfront billing. Crèches are available at gyms, community centres and at some places of work too, so have a look and see what's available near you.

Childminders are an alternative to nursery and may be more flexible, although not necessarily. They are running a business too and need to adhere to legal ratios of child to adult so they need to know in advance how many children are coming to them each day. But many don't work to full capacity and may be able to fit you in on an ad hoc basis.

You could get a nanny or live-in au pair. Obviously, this option will depend on your income level but don't immediately rule it out as being too expensive. If you have more than one child or your job requires you to be home later than a nursery closes, then it might be easier than taking your child to and from nursery. Nanny shares are possible with two or three parents 'sharing' a nanny to bring costs down. Don't forget with nannies that you are employing them (rather than the business–customer relationship you have with a childminder) so you'll need to adhere to tax and pension requirements if you go down this route.

At the age of two or three your child will become eligible for a free nursery place. You can claim this nursery place at a nursery or childminder, as long as they are registered with Ofsted, and the government will pay money directly to the institution claiming. The money is for term time only (38 weeks) and you usually need to renew your claim at the start of each term. So, if you're sending your child to a nursery which carries on throughout the school holidays, be aware that you won't get your free hours during those weeks. However, some nurseries will spread the allowance over the whole year so each month works out roughly the same for you. When you sign up with a nursery, check how they work it out and whether you can do term time only or must commit to 52 weeks a year.

Childcare is perhaps the trickiest of all practicalities to sort out as you have to take into account the costs and timings, but also your child's happiness. You may be lucky enough to find the perfect childminder living in your street or you may have to walk miles to a nursery which you're still not convinced by. Remember that, just like your work decision, childcare arrangements can be changed if they're not working out for you or your child. In the meantime, be open to ideas and look for all the options open to you – speaking to other parents is a good way to get recommendations for childcare settings or ideas about unusual arrangements.

TIME MANAGEMENT

Whether you go back to work, start a business or stay at home with the kids, time management is crucial. The experience you get when you become a mum will set you up perfectly for the obstacles, distractions and skills you need to manage your time effectively in your work life.

Before I had kids I thought that I was pretty good at time management. I was the kind of person who was always on time to work, barring some major incident, and, apart from a bit of a tendency to leave things until the last minute, I was generally okay at managing my time.

But, that said, I also wasn't a hugely organised person. Despite my job in project management (I still don't know how I ever ended up there), I wasn't the kind of person who made lists for everything, alphabetised their CD collection or colour coded their wardrobe. I wasn't scatty or untidy, but I didn't feel that so much in my life required organising either. I mostly winged it.

Then I became a mum of twins and everything changed.

I kept lists of when the babies ate and slept and pooed. I had columns for poo colour and consistency. They weren't breastfeeding so I was monitoring how many millilitres of formula they were drinking and how many times a day. There was a practical use to it all though. Writing stuff down meant I didn't get them mixed up and feed one twice or something stupid, which was perfectly possible given the average two hours of broken sleep I was getting each night. But more than the practical use for the information, I just needed it out of my head. I needed to not have to try and remember anything because there was so much going on.

So I became a bit listy. And because getting out of the house was such a mission I also developed ways to make it easier, like packing the changing bag the night before, making sure I had wipes wherever I went and always having several spare pairs of socks to replace the random ones which the babies removed and dropped over the side of the buggy when I wasn't looking. Being disorganised just wasn't an option – I had to sort this stuff out.

If you've already had a job where you were pretty autonomous and you decided what work you did at what time, then you may think that going back to it after having kids, or starting your own business, probably won't require many more time management skills than you already have. In some ways that's true, but if you're tying in your working day with nursery pick ups, or getting home at a certain time so that your partner can go out, or working out how to build a freelance career around parenting, you'll be mixing the domestic with the professional in new ways.

You're in great company, though, because lots of women have done this and continue to do this. For instance, when I was doing copywriting I was once in a Skype video call with a client when my kids came in unexpectedly (they'd been out of the house with their dad and had come home earlier than expected). Suddenly my client got interrupted by an excitable four-year-old wanting to climb on Mummy. As it happens, being a business mum herself, the client wasn't at all perturbed and after a little shushing and a quick cuddle, my son was back with his dad in the other room and we were able to resume our call.

Had that happened when I was working as a consultant and on a video call to a room full of people in a traditional office setting, I would have come across as unprofessional. You know as well as I do that professionalism is really about how well you do your work, and whether you're doing it with babies in the next room or from a super swanky penthouse office suite makes no difference to your ability and skills, but your clients may not always see it that way. Which is why when I chose my copywriting clients I purposefully looked for businesses run by mums, because those are the kind of businesses that I like to work with. It doesn't have to be mum-run businesses though – small businesses in general are more likely to be sympathetic to a supplier who wants to do the work for them in the evening or at weekends or who may have other demands on their time and is weaving the domestic and professional together.

I don't resonate with the dry corporate background from whence I came so I don't seek out clients who are like that. It made my life harder to try and mask the reality of my work set up, which for many people starting out doesn't even include a dedicated office – it's more likely to be a laptop sat on the sofa or a computer desk in the corner of the living room. It's so much easier to run your business when you can be honest that that's the way it is for you and that you may only be working 10 hours a week while your baby is still young.

If you are going to be working at home, whether for yourself or for an employer, the biggest time management advice I can offer is to work out which tasks you need to do and split them into those that you can do with your baby around – perhaps checking emails from your smartphone while your baby has a little nap or outlining a presentation you have to do – and those that you need to do when you're fully focused and your baby is down for the night or being looked after by someone else. Then, when that someone else is looking after your baby, do the most important stuff first. Don't faff around doing the dishes, scrolling through Facebook or reading emails – write a blog post, put together a proposal for a potential client or create the presentation slides. Kids can be unpredictable and you'll kick yourself if you've got the house straight and are just about to start on your work when you get a call from nursery to pick up your sick child.

In addition, don't spend any of that precious time deciding what to do – you should already know. Have things set up so that when you get half an hour, either expectedly or unexpectedly, you know exactly what the next thing is that you're going to work on. If you're working in 30-minute chunks and you spend 10 minutes deciding what to do, starting up your laptop and logging into your website, then you only have 20 minutes left to actually work.

This is the reality of running a business or working from home with children. You need to be organised, plan more in advance and be more prepared for distractions than you ever would have been in your day job. But that doesn't make it impossible. And, in fact, if you're a new mum you'll be discovering how most of this stuff comes far more naturally than it did ever before.

CASE STUDY

Her story

Being a working mum is a constant juggle and even more so when you are the boss. I am one of those people who desperately believes that anything is possible and, because I believed that it was possible to run a big business around the short school hours, I have cracked on and made it happen. My business turns over six figures, but it is run by part-time mums. We have it set up so that we are very flexible about how we work and our babies come first every step of the way. I believe that, when you are a mum in business, you need to adopt a totally different approach than you may be used to in a corporate environment. Trying to work the same long hours and adhere to the rules set by those expectations simply adds to our stress, and the more stress we have on our shoulders as a mum, the more stress our children experience.

I feel so lucky to be able to work three days a week with a few hours on a Monday afternoon too. I am able to work like this as I have lots of automation and systems set up in my business, so I know that when I am not there, everything is still being answered and sorted: a task that may normally take four hours can be done in 30 minutes with the use of clever tools. The key is learning how to boost your productivity and also to try and switch off in between working times so when you do work you will be at your best. You need to plan your time carefully so when you sit down to work you know exactly what you need to do. Often we can find ourselves becoming overwhelmed and this is when we lose the little time we do have and become stressed. By investing in the right technology, creating systems and starting to outsource the bits which are not playing to your strengths, you are able to build as big a business as someone dedicating six days a week to something. In this day and age, it is not about working harder, it is about working smarter.

Victoria Casebourne, TheKeepsakeCo.co.uk

INVESTING IN YOURSELF

Many women find investing in themselves very difficult. For a number of reasons, mostly to do with low self-esteem or a lack of inner confidence, these women find themselves making do or doing stuff on the cheap. Having a baby affects people in different ways, but for someone lacking in self-esteem it's quite likely that it will knock their confidence even more, leading them to put other people's desires before their own and not seek out the support they need. This section could sit just as comfortably in the following chapter on mental and emotional headspace, but I've put it here because it's so closely linked to money.

Many of us make the decision about what to do after maternity leave based only on what we believe our financial situation to be, rather than viewing our choice as an investment in ourselves and our family for the future. Investing in ourselves is so important because it gives us the support, knowledge or confidence we need to achieve something. That might mean spending money on new clothes or a smart new handbag so that you feel professional rather than frumpy when you return to work; or on practical non-office clothes if you're going to be a full-time mum (just because you may spend a lot of time inside and cleaning doesn't mean you have to dress like Cinderella). I'm not saying to chuck out the budget, but you've probably bought yourself new clothes for a new job before, so give yourself the same treatment when your new job is becoming a mum.

It's obviously not all about clothes, though. If you've decided to start a business, don't do it apologetically, signing up for all the free versions of software and only learning from free webinars or e-courses that cost less than a tenner. It costs money to run a business and, if you're learning as you're going along, then you should invest in that learning. Sure, there are loads of free tools out there which can be very useful and it's great to trial something so that you know it's worth your while to buy it (or not), but don't carry forward the mind-set of getting everything for free or cheap once you start getting some money into your business.

That said, don't use investing in yourself as an excuse not to succeed either. If you dig around a little in the online business space you'll find hundreds of coaches and e-courses on launching new products, designing e-courses, running marketing or social media campaigns, getting your message across, finding your message, managing self-care or self-confidence, speaking in public, writing for your business, monetising podcasts … Seriously, whatever stage you reach in your business and think *'I need to learn how to do this'*, there will be a course out there for it. The trick is identifying only those courses that you need. I know people who have spent thousands of pounds on e-courses over the last few years and still don't have a business to show for it because they've convinced themselves that they'll only be qualified to start after the next course.

Investing in yourself and your business is necessary but

you don't have to go overboard. You don't have to spend thousands before you've made a penny and you don't have to learn everything before you start. Instead, make a plan. Work out what you need to learn. Also, work out if it's more cost-effective (in terms of both time and money) to learn it or to hire in someone with the expertise. It's pointless spending a few hundred quid and a couple of weeks away from client work, for instance, to immerse yourself in learning the ins and outs of Facebook advertising. It would probably be cheaper and quicker to spend the same amount of money on hiring someone who already knows it. And this goes for any specialist area in business – copywriting, social media management, podcast editing, and so on. Some things you can and will want to do yourself, but with others it's a false economy to make yourself an expert in something that only needs doing once or rarely.

As with all things in life, it's about balance and your attitude to the situation. Don't refuse to spend money on your business because you think it won't work out anyway – that's a self-fulfilling prophecy. Likewise, don't throw all your savings at something in the blind belief that if you invest enough it'll all work out. Do your research, listen to your intuition and, where possible, work up gradually, ensuring you earn some money from the business before investing a bit more.

If you're returning to work or being a full-time mum, the same advice applies. Think about what you need in terms of learning, equipment or accessories and go out there and get it. Don't apologise for needing something in order to do your role effectively and don't use money as an excuse for why something didn't work out.

Finally, if you have a partner, speak to them about money. If they believe you're spending it frivolously then they aren't going to be supportive of your plans. Sometimes this will be their own hang-ups and doubts about the risks of running a business or the realities of how much it costs for childcare or kids' activities, and other times it will be a valid point they raise. Don't get defensive. You need their support, whether you're starting up a business or adjusting the family budget to take into consideration your new role as a full-time mum.

Above all, remember you deserve whatever you want, so make sure that the choices you make are right for you and not based purely on finances or someone else's idea of what your future career should look like.

Here I have talked specifically about spending money on yourself and on your future plans. The next chapter will give you more general tools and advice for keeping your mind healthy.

CHAPTER 8

Mental and Emotional Headspace

As you've probably gathered by now, whether you're already a mum or still pregnant, life with a little one is wildly different to your life before they came along. We get on and deal with all the practical stuff because we have to, but how often do we give ourselves the time to come to terms emotionally and mentally with everything that's changing in our lives? It's vital to look after our mental health just as we would our physical health, especially now we have the responsibility of being a mum.

MIND-SET

The mind-set we hold encroaches on all areas of our lives and it's impossible to make any kind of life decision, like what to do about your career after maternity leave, without understanding where our heads are at.

Your mind-set consists of your assumptions about yourself,

your attitude towards what you want to achieve and also the mental blocks that you put up all around you, completely subconsciously, which stop you achieving those things.

MY EXPERIENCE

It's probably worth sharing a bit of my own story here to illustrate just how relevant your mind-set is to your choices. At the time of writing this book I've been self-employed for four years and my income has gone steadily downhill since my first year. You'd think I'd be too ashamed of that fact to share it, but far from it. I consider my life much better now than it was four years ago, partly because I no longer link my income level to my self-worth and partly because I measure success by how happy I am to have had a certain experience in my life, rather than what I've gained from it materially.

The background story is that during those four years I went from being a self-employed consultant in London working on knowledge management projects in global organisations while my husband did most of the childcare at home, to living in Cornwall, being separated, then divorced, and for the last three years being solely responsible for two children and their childcare.

So, there were clearly practical reasons why my earning potential dropped, but more importantly than those were my psychological reasons. Once I'd moved to Cornwall there was something about being so far from the City that made me completely disinterested in the field I used to consult in. Once I was free of the smog and the morning commute, I wanted to create a new life rather than trying to cling on to my old one. I was happy to send my smart black suits and high heels to charity shops or the bin, and find a completely different way of earning money. Moving to Cornwall had a massive transformative effect on me, as did becoming a lone parent. Just like my priorities changed when I became a mother, so they changed again when I became a single mother.

For a lot of the past three years I've been quite undecided about what I wanted from this new life, and so even though I've had good and lucrative months in my various business ventures, I've often lacked focus, motivation and commitment which have led to bad months too. Because I can see the link between my focus and motivation and the results I get, and because of the many personal development courses I've done and coaching sessions I've had, I know that these are essential factors for success.

Sometimes mental blocks have arisen because I was on the wrong track – like when I couldn't muster the energy or enthusiasm to continue with my consulting career. I wasn't in the right frame of mind to succeed on that path and I took that as an indication that I needed to move on to something else. In comparison, sometimes I've found myself procrastinating over a task and after a bit of soul-searching I've identified that I was doubting my ability to do it well. Once I knew that it was self-doubt that was causing me to put it off, and not an underlying feeling that I shouldn't be doing it at all, I had to overcome the block and push through.

Resistance to doing something is an excellent indicator that you need to look more deeply at what it is you're resisting and work out why that is. Lack of focus is another, and of course procrastination. Likewise, don't ignore gut feelings, hunches or that feeling of dread you get every morning before work. Our minds do a lot of work beneath the surface and behaviours and feelings like these are one way of understanding what we're thinking at a deeper level.

As you can imagine, I'm only touching the surface here. There are whole books dedicated to the issue of mindset and mental attitude and they'll obviously cover it in more detail than I can. But I am going to talk about motivation in a little more detail because this will give you the strong foundation on which to build a big career change or to deal with the normal everyday process of re-evaluating your priorities now you're a parent.

MOTIVATION

What is motivating you to read this book right now? I suspect it's because you want to make a conscious decision about your future career now that you are having kids. That's a pretty strong motivation. Enough for you to buy the book and invest time in reading it. So, you're motivated enough to invest a few quid and few hours of your time to the question. But then what next? Hopefully something you've read in these pages coupled with your own reflection and experience will lead you to a decision or at least some ideas to try out. That's when your motivation is going to be properly tested. So best to work out now where you stand.

For many of us our motivation for going to work is really just the obligation of it. We have a job and, unless we want to get sacked and potentially ruin our life, we just get up every morning and go to work. We may have been motivated by other factors to apply for the job, but once we're there the biggest motivation is just duty and probably necessity in the form of the money we're being paid to be there too.

For some lucky ones, their motivation is more than just obligation. They love their work. They choose to work more hours than they're paid for, not out of a sense of obligation, but out of a sense of love, fulfilment and enjoyment. They live for the work they do and they can't imagine doing anything else. If you're not one of these people, wouldn't it be a wonderful state to aspire to when you plan your future career?

Before you make any decision about your future it's wise to figure out what motivates you in your current job, in your past jobs and in your hobbies and interests. Parenthood has a funny habit of turning your motivations and priorities upside down, so take that into account too.

WHAT IS YOUR WHY?

In every introduction to starting a business that I've ever seen is the question 'What is your why?' It is an excellent question, which is probably why business coaches ask it all the time. What is your why? Why are you doing this? And it's not just relevant to people starting a business; it's relevant to everyone to ask themselves about their chosen work or job. The reason to ask this question is to give you a statement of intent – a statement which, when you're feeling low or lacking in confidence, you can look at to pep you up and remind you why you're here and why you started this journey.

Maybe you're doing this because you want to spend time with your baby. Or because you've never earned much money before and now you feel it is time to step it up a gear and start providing more for your family. Maybe you want to move to a certain place in the world. Maybe your why is about giving your children a role model of a working mum or a successful mum. Perhaps you want to be successful because you feel you've failed at something in the past. Maybe you've been successful in your career thus far but it doesn't light you up and you want to use a different skill or talent instead.

These are just ideas and things I've heard from talking to others. Your why is specific to you. You need to work it out on your own. One way to start this process is to consider what would happen if you didn't do this business / work / job. What would you be missing out on? What do you feel you can't achieve any other way?

One thing that doesn't work very well is a simple money goal. If you think your why is to make a certain amount of money it may not be very motivating because, when the going gets tough, you might just decide there are easier ways to make the money. So although making a certain amount of money might be *part* of your why, the money goal on its own with no context or motivation is not really a 'why'.

Think:

- Why this business, this job or this course?
- Why now?
- Why not that other thing?

Use these questions to really drill down into why you're doing this and not something else. Play devil's advocate and demand difficult answers from yourself. Once you've got this worked out, this becomes the foundation for your business or for your work, and your motivation when things get hard.

Aside from knowing why you're doing it, it's also worth revisiting your ambition, both in the past and now:

- What did you want to do when you grew up?
- What ambitions did you have then? And since?
- Are you harbouring a deep-seated desire to be recognised for your work in some specific way? Or to do certain work in the first place?

- Do you consider yourself ambitious?
- Is financial success important to you?

Again, there are no right or wrong answers but you do need to link all these things to you and what you're doing.

For instance, if financial success has always been important to you in the past, and if that's still the case after you've had children, then you need this to be part of your life. You probably won't be satisfied with a business that only brings in pocket money, or as a full-time mum, or taking a large pay cut in order to work fewer hours. I'm certainly not saying you should define yourself by your earning potential, but if you've always been that way and becoming a mother hasn't changed it, then make it a factor in your decision rather than hoping you'll change your values spontaneously.

Likewise, if you've never cared much about money and you're the kind of person who feels they can get by on just a little and anything more is excessive, then don't start the kind of business which is focused purely on numbers and profit but where you don't resonate with the product or service. And don't take on a high-paid role which doesn't really move you in any other way. The money won't motivate you for long and you'll get bored or disillusioned with what you're trying to achieve.

Knowing your why and what you want to achieve out of life will give you a powerful motivational boost at those times when you need it most: when you can't seem to find the time to get your work done, you're procrastinating or when you've had a knock-back, a rejection or something hasn't worked out in the way you planned. Your motivational boost will keep you pushing on through the hard times and keep you positive when things aren't running smoothly.

BE YOURSELF

I talked about the fear of losing your identity briefly in Chapter 4, but it's a universal fear for any new mums no matter what career step they take afterwards, so I want to revisit it.

Becoming a parent is a huge life change. One minute you're responsible for only yourself, perhaps sharing responsibility for mortgage or rent payments on your house and earning money; basically being an adult. Then you have a baby. And you're 100 per cent responsible for another life. And not just for keeping the life surviving with food and good hygiene, but committing to a future of educating, supporting and unconditionally loving this other life. No wonder it feels overwhelming for most people.

The first time I took my twins home from the hospital I had this sudden feeling of everything I knew being ripped out from under me and the realisation that I was now in charge. I felt the same feeling the first time I was alone in the house with them. At that moment, I didn't feel like myself at all – I felt like a completely different person. Feelings like this vary from person to person and mostly come and go as quickly as a flash, but they all add up to making you feel not quite yourself during the first few days, weeks, and even months, of your baby's life.

Then, when you've got used to being a mum and you start thinking about your work and what you're going to do next, you may find that you feel quite differently about a lot of things. Your priorities shift forward and back and side to side at this time. One day you might be dying to get back to work while the next you just want to put on an apron and bake bread and cakes for the rest of your life. Your job, which once you loved so much, may suddenly lack meaning and you can't imagine yourself back there. Or you have renewed ambition to climb the corporate ladder and leave your colleagues in your wake. Some people become more sure of what they want while others become less sure of absolutely everything they once thought unquestionable. All reactions are normal, and one of the great things about maternity leave is having the opportunity to feel them and not judge yourself before making any decisions about your career.

It's not as simple as saying, if you're the domestic type then be a full-time mum or if you're the cerebral type then you should go back to work. Nothing is as cut and dry as that. There are plenty of people who are not 'typical' examples of their job or who surprise others when they share what they do for a living.

Identity is a funny thing. On the one hand, we look for something to define us, but very often when we find ourselves defined by a certain identity we rebel against it. Being a mum is a wonderful identity, but it's only part of who you are and who you will become. Everything changes. Add the mum identity to everything else you know about yourself, and move on and grow.

What about everyone else? How do they define you and how do you think they see you? It doesn't matter. The choices you make now about your direction in life are for you to make, together with your partner if you have one. It doesn't matter whether your dad wants you to continue being a lawyer or your sister wants you to be a full-time mum like her so you can do stuff together during the day. Everyone has their own plans and ideas for you, and you need to find some way to stay grounded and be yourself.

Which is a lot easier if you're not also comparing yourself to everyone else. It's perfectly natural to do so, though. We compare ourselves to others all the time. I see other people's posts on social media about the cool activities they're doing with their kids and I wish I had thought of doing that. I wish I spent more time making fairy cakes for my kids or home-made ice lollies. I talk to the other mums about what they did at the weekend and I think we should have done something other than what we did. I see a friend getting promoted and I wonder whether I should have stayed on in my old job.

You have to let all of this go. Because you can only be yourself. Yes, you can try new things and get better at others, but don't try and force yourself into not being yourself by doing stuff you don't enjoy and don't really care about, other than to keep up with the others you see doing it.

It's your life and your decision.

YOUR RELATIONSHIP WITH YOUR PARTNER

Becoming a parent changes everyone in some way, so it makes sense that when two people becoming parents at the same time, it is bound to have an impact on their relationship. I'm sure most people could write a book on how their relationship changed once kids came along. Although it's not the main focus of this book, it is relevant because it impacts hugely on your career decision. Because for everything I've said about your identity and your choices and being yourself, they are only part of the jigsaw puzzle. What your partner wants is a big part of it too. Might he want to give up work and become a full-time dad, for instance? Have you asked him?

Hopefully most couples will have had this discussion either before getting pregnant or at least before the baby is born, but sometimes these discussions take time. It may take weeks or months for you to get clear on what you actually want and that goes for your partner too. Just because he says when you first get pregnant that he'd never want to be a full-time dad doesn't mean he won't change his mind once he actually becomes a parent. If not a full-time dad, perhaps he might be up for one or two days a week as primary carer, allowing you both to work part-time and incur little to no childcare costs.

MATERNITY LEAVERS

The possibilities and combinations are endless and specific to each couple based on your income levels, seniority in your organisations, whether you have family around to help or not, and any number of other variables. But I can't stress enough that it all begins with a conversation and will probably involve lots of conversations. Both of you need to listen to the other and know what each other's hopes and dreams are for the future. Perhaps your husband doesn't like his job but he stays in it because it pays well. Maybe he dreams of one day moving to Cornwall and opening his own surf school. Maybe you also fancy the beach life and would rather ditch your London flat for a light and airy attic room with a view of the sea and a life of writing books. Or something completely different. What matters is that now you're a parenting team, you need to know each other's motivations as well as your strengths and weaknesses.

So what are each of you good at? Maybe one of you is a bit of a night owl and could easily deal with waking up at night, whereas the other doesn't mind getting up super early and would deal much better with a 5am call for breakfast. Maybe one of you is practical and creative and brilliant at thinking up rainy day craft activities with the kids, while the other would happily lead an expedition into the woods on a crisp autumn day. Everyone is good at something and, likewise, we're all a bit rubbish at other things. Try to divvy out housework and childcare duties based on each other's strengths and what you like doing, so that you don't both end up resenting each other because you're doing exactly the kind of things you hate.

Parenting in a relationship is about teamwork and sometimes compromise. Take time to learn about each other before making any life decisions, and keep up that dialogue when you're in the thick of it so you can flag up stuff that isn't working and things that need changing.

As I mentioned in Chapter 4, the income dynamics may alter significantly once you become a family. Talk about this too. Don't let resentments rise about who is working or who is earning.

Above all, remember this is a new situation for you both, and you both deserve the opportunity to create your own ideal career and lifestyle.

Conclusion

WHAT TO DO NOW…

Now that you've reached the end of the book, what's next?

I hope that some of the ideas or advice in this book have helped you and made it clearer on what career steps you want to take next, or at least not feel so overwhelmed by the choices on offer to you (or despairing of a lack of them).

There are a few things I've said in the course of the book which I feel are worth emphasising:

- **Plans, choices and decisions can all be changed if you need or want to.** You only need to formulate a plan for the foreseeable future and after that, review, regroup, renegotiate, whatever. Don't become so wedded to a decision that you can't or won't change it even when all the evidence points to the fact that it's not working out.
- **There are always more options than you think.** Hopefully I've put forward a few that you haven't thought of, but now you're in the swing of it, perhaps you can think of a few more that I didn't think of.
- **Don't over research.** By all means, check out legal requirements or personal stories when you have an idea of something you'd like to do, but don't use the need for research be an excuse to put off trying something or to put you off an idea altogether.
- **Only you can decide what is right for you.** Talk to friends, family and colleagues, and by all means, take their views and advice into account, but don't base your

final decision on what other people think you should do. And don't judge other mums for the decisions they make either. Let's all be nice and supportive to each other.

- **If you're in a relationship this is a joint decision, so don't shoulder it all on your own.** Your partner may not be aware of all the options open to him as a father, so if you want him to take a bigger role in the family and childcare, talk to him about doing so and support him if he decides to apply for parental leave.

Finally, don't lose sight of your dreams. Maternity leave is the perfect time to reconnect with yourself and bring the dreams and goals you've buried, during your day-to-day life and career, back to the surface. Nurture your baby but don't forget to nurture yourself too.

Resources

Benefits Calculators
https://www.gov.uk/benefits-calculators

Childcare Costs
http://www.familyandchildcaretrust.org/sites/default/files/files/Childcare_cost_survey_2015_Final.pdf

http://www.babycentre.co.uk/a552732/the-cost-of-childcare

http://www.which.co.uk/reviews/childcare/article/childcare-in-the-uk/how-much-does-childcare-cost

GOV.UK
https://www.gov.uk/

Maternity Action
https://www.maternityaction.org.uk/
Advice Line: 0845 600 85 33

Job Websites for Mums
http://workingmums.co.uk
https://www.2to3days.com/
http://mumandworking.co.uk

How To Become A Huffington Post Blogger (my own article)
http://bit.ly/soozihuffpo

Online Journaling
http://penzu.com
http://750words.com

Matched Betting
http://bit.ly/soozimatchedbetting

Links and further information about all the resources I've mentioned throughout the book are on the Maternity Leavers website: www.maternityleavers.com

I'll update this website regularly with other resources I didn't mention and anything else I find that I think will be helpful for you.